# TO BE A KING

# TO BE A KING

## Dermot Morrah

ARUNDEL HERALD EXTRAORDINARY

A privileged account of the early life and education of H.R.H. the Prince of Wales, written with the approval of H.M. the Queen

HUTCHINSON OF LONDON

HUTCHINSON & CO *(Publishers)* LTD
*178–202 Great Portland Street, London W1*

London Melbourne Sydney
Auckland Bombay Toronto
Johannesburg New York

★

*First published 1968*

*This book has been set in Bembo, printed in Great Britain
on Antique Wove paper by Anchor Press, and
bound by Wm. Brendon, both of Tiptree, Essex*

09 084940 x

# CONTENTS

# ACKNOWLEDGEMENTS

My thanks are due in fourfold measure to Her Majesty the Queen for permission to attempt this study of the childhood and education of His Royal Highness the Prince of Wales; for all the special facilities granted me; for the loan of the numerous family photographs; and for Her Majesty's generous help.

I am also deeply indebted to the Prince of Wales himself for his personal assistance.

Finally I am grateful to all those others who, by their patience and co-operation in the collection of material, have assisted in the production of this book. I have relied on them for most of my information and have given great weight to their opinions in forming my own. Nevertheless for all judgments expressed in the following pages, as for any errors of fact, which I fear I cannot have wholly escaped, I bear the sole responsibility.

D.M.M.M.

# ILLUSTRATIONS

# ILLUSTRATIONS

*The reproduction of the family photographs in this book (marked above by an asterisk) is by kind permission of the Queen. Their copyright is reserved.*

INTRODUCTION

# SOVEREIGN AND HEIR

O F ALL forms of human society on earth, hereditary
monarchy is the most universal in time, though no
longer the most widely distributed in space. As far back as
we can peer into the recesses of prehistory, tribes and nations
have wished to see son, or occasionally daughter, succeeding
father in the most conspicuous, the symbolic, place. Some
great peoples in antiquity, a few in the Middle Ages, many
in modern times, have discarded the system in favour of
republican forms. There remain nevertheless in 1968 some
sixty hereditary monarchs, ranging from the Queen of the
United Kingdom, Head of the Commonwealth, and the
Mikado of Japan to the Prince of Monaco and the Sheikhs
of the Persian Gulf. In particular, the four great nations of
British stock, Great Britain, Canada, Australia and New
Zealand, continue to place their faith in the venerable
system, believing on the basis of their long and continuous
history that this—whatever may be appropriate to the
different circumstances of other nations—is the most satis-
factory social order for themselves.

Of the many advantages of the hereditary principle, some
of which may become apparent as this story progresses, the

most obvious to the plain man is that it enables the future
sovereign to be known from childhood and deliberately
trained for his high office. It is possible to achieve this
advantage in some other systems. For example, the Tibetans
believe that at the moment of the death of their Dalai Lama
his spirit becomes incarnate in some new-born baby boy,
whom it is the business of their astrologers to find and
identify, in order that he may be brought up to fill the
vacant place. In fact, they do not believe that the place is
ever vacant: there is only one Dalai Lama, living throughout
history and only changing his bodily shape from time to
time. We cannot go so far as that; but to us also the idea of
continuity is indispensable. We give our allegiance, age by
age, not to the same being but to the same family, handing
down the torch from generation to generation. Thus we
hope to ensure that the ideas and ideals by which we live,
and of which the personality of the man or woman on the
Throne is the symbolic expression, preserve both their
permanent indestructible essence and their power to develop,
as we ourselves develop, from age to age without a break.

For this idea of royal continuity goes deeper than the
evident advantage of placing at the head of society a person
who has qualified for that position by specialized training
and not by success in a struggle with rival aspirants. From
the remotest period the king has always been above all else
the universal representative of his people, the emblematic
figure in whom their corporate life is concentrated and
made visible. This is an idea much older than authority; for
it does not seem that power was an important element,
perhaps even an element at all, in the origin of kings. The
prehistoric king may have been identified with the crops by
which the tribe lived, or with the totem beast of their cult;
he may have been a sacrificing priest, undoubtedly there are
many instances where he was destined to end as a human
sacrifice himself; there was something in him of the magi-

cian, something of the mascot, something of the god. It is comparatively late in time that he became a ruler—and he may cease to rule and still be a king. But one thing he can never cease to be, and that is a representative. In the continental homelands of our Anglo-Saxon ancestors—so constitutional historians tell us—the first kings were consecrated beings, standing for the unity of the tribe but in no sense governing it. By the time they invaded Britain they had become captains of war; very tentatively thereafter they became interpreters of the customary law and so eventually law-givers; with the feudal system came the idea that the king is the universal landlord; the Tudors took to themselves supreme spiritual power and bequeathed to the Stuarts the conception of 'the Prince' as the autocrat whose commands are law. Then began the reaction. The immense concentration of power in the hands of the benevolent despots of the Renaissance has been steadily redistributed, first to the landed aristocracy, then to the middle classes, until today it is shared by the whole body of the people. But although in Great Britain the Sovereign is left with very little personal power over the State—as distinct from persuasive influence which may be profound—this does not mean that there has been a decline of the monarchy. What has declined is its political authority, a thing of which we can see in history the rise and diminution, a thing added to the fundamental concept and capable of being subtracted without damage thereto. As the political aspect of the monarchy has dwindled, the need for it as the expression of the nation's ideals has become more visible. It has indeed been refreshed from the original fount of its being, the need implanted in human nature for some inspiring personality to which all may look up as the figure in whom all are incarnate, by whom all—not the majority but all—are represented.

At all times in history, therefore, the ideal guiding prin-

ciple in the upbringing of a future king is that his education
should be directed to making him a representative man of
his age. His age, be it remembered, is not the age of the
reigning Sovereign whose heir he is. His age is the future;
and it is necessary therefore that his education be planned
with an imaginative eye to the way in which the people
over whom he is to reign is likely to develop in character and
outlook. This ideal has not always been realized. In the last
century and a half, and very recently, the criticism brought
against monarchy is that it is an excessively conservative
influence, tending always to perpetuate the values of the age
that is dying. This is an influence that is perhaps most
dangerous when it affects the training of young princes;
they may be confined within the hothouse atmosphere of
palaces and grow up out of touch with their young contemporaries, whose inarticulate thoughts and emotions it
will hereafter be their business to interpret. 'Will you,
the youth of the British Commonwealth and Empire,' said
the present Queen in her coming-of-age broadcast, 'allow
me to speak on my birthday as your representative?'
Nobody thought this an extravagant claim, because Princess
Elizabeth, Second Subaltern in the A.T.S., had become a
familiar figure and was known to have enthusiastically
shared the normal wartime experiences of girls of her age.
There have been heirs in the past from whom the words
would have sounded ridiculous.

Yet there is a contrasting side to the picture. Those responsible for the education of a future king must not follow
after every new trend merely because it is new, if only
because there are always many conflicting trends, and it
requires rare and profound judgment to determine with
which of them the future really lies. Moreover, nobody
knows how long the heir will be occupying that position.
Heirs Apparent have acceded at all ages from the few
months of Henry VI to the near sixty of Edward VII. A

theological seminary or a military academy may design the training of an ordinand or a cadet in the reasonable certainty that he will not be bearing the responsibility of a bishop or a general within the next quarter of a century. But the heir to the Throne may be called to the highest place at any moment; and although, should he accede before the age of eighteen, his formal powers will be temporarily exercised for him by a Regent, the mystical reverence that surrounds a king will begin to attach to his person in the public mind from the very first. He is always, even as a child, in some sort the understudy to the reigning Sovereign; and the possibility of his being unexpectedly required to play the leading part cannot be wholly lost to sight at any stage of his education.

The heir, so long as he remains the heir, is in a peculiar sense the supreme representative of the rising generation. Perhaps it would be more accurate to speak of his own generation; for when, as sometimes happens, he becomes a grandfather while still Prince of Wales, he may well find the symbolic leadership of the youth of the nation passing to his own son. But the heir, whether young or middle-aged, is at all times in a special sense the representative figure in the age group to which he himself belongs. When he becomes king he necessarily becomes the universal representative, standing not for any group in the nation but for the whole. He will indeed represent something more than the whole body of the living people over whom he reigns. By virtue of the hereditary principle he will be the connecting link between the glory of the past and the hopes of the future; for one of the essential elements in the concept of monarchy is the idea of continuity. Looking to the royal family, not as discrete public figures like Prime Ministers succeeding according to the ebb and flow of party politics, but as a single line of human beings of one blood extending through history, to whom their ancestors known and unknown have given allegiance, the people are helped to feel their own identity with the whole national tradition of the past, and indeed with the nation as it will become when they themselves are ancestors. For the descendants of their reigning monarch will still stand as the representative of the yet unborn.

Here then is the second indispensable theme in the education of a future king. It must be directed with an imaginative eye to the future; yet it must be firmly anchored in the experience of the past. It must look to the inevitability of change as reign follows reign; yet it must conceive change always as organic growth and not as revolution. The problem of balancing these forces in the education of a prince has always been present: it arises out of the timeless nature of monarchy, as the visible emblem of a nation's ideal, and not out of its changing relation to the business of state.

Many and various are the solutions that bygone Kings and Queens of England have devised to meet the changing circumstances of a thousand years; and most of these are glanced at in the historical appendix beginning on p. 161. Directly or indirectly all this long experience underlies the upbringing of the present heir of 1968.

# PRINCE CHARLES OF
# EDINBURGH

THE story begins on a grey November day in 1948. The crowd had been deepening along the railings ever since dawn, attracted by last night's news that Sir William Gilliatt, the gynaecologist, had decided to remain at Buckingham Palace. During the morning tension mounted with the discovery that Sir John Weir, the King's physician, had arrived and both doctors were presumably seeing the twenty-two-year-old Princess Elizabeth, Duchess of Edinburgh—but the excitement ebbed a little later when the gates opened for Sir John to drive out again. After-lunch strollers made their way through the quiet Sunday streets and took up vantage points around the Victoria Memorial— on the steps at first; later they would try climbing up the statuary when the police were not looking, though there was nothing in particular to be seen. Others arrived in cars, which they parked along the Mall.

Soon after dusk, the midwife, Sister Helen Rowe, called Sir William to the Princess's room. A few minutes later, the Duke accompanied his wife to the Buhl Room, once part of the royal children's quarters, but more recently transformed into a surgical ward for an operation on the arteries of the

King's leg. The Duke, always restless in times of waiting, changed into flannels and a roll-collar sweater and went down to the Palace squash court with his friend and private secretary, Lieutenant-Commander Michael Parker, formerly of the Royal Australian Navy. Outside, the police interrupted their attempts to keep a space clear for the guardsmen marching up and down on their beat, and began to wave and jostle the crowd back to make way for the cars bringing Sir John Weir again—this time followed by Mr. Peel and Mr. Hall, the gynaecologist and anaesthetist from King's College Hospital. The watchers numbered three or four thousand now, intent for every sign, but making little noise.

The Duke was still down in the squash court when news came that the baby had been born. He hurried to the sitting room where the King and Queen were waiting and then on to the Buhl Room near by. The Princess had not yet come round from the anaesthetic. He ran on to the nursery to take his first look at the baby, and then back to the sitting room, where the new grandparents had their first opportunity to congratulate him, the King shaking his hand and the Queen embracing him. He led them to the nursery to admire their grandchild; and when the Princess regained consciousness he was standing beside her bed with a large bouquet of roses and carnations in his hand. Later he returned to the sitting room to open bottles of champagne for the doctors and Household officers, while the messages went out to friends, relations, Governors and Ambassadors, from the post office inside the Palace, the first of them, according to the ancient privilege of the City, addressed to the Lord Mayor of London.

An attendant came out of the Palace and spoke to a policeman. The policeman spoke to those nearest to him along the railings. The word flew from one to the next, whispered, spoken, shouted. By the time Queen Mary's car arrived, bringing her up from Marlborough House, the merry-making was in full swing. Choruses of 'For He's a Jolly Good Fellow' greeted a tall fair-haired figure that crossed the forecourt and was enthusiastically mistaken for the baby's father. At eleven o'clock a copy of the Court Circular was posted by the railings. In knots, eddies and arrowheads, the crowd elbowed around it, their numbers doubled by now. An hour later the gates opened for a car to drive out. The path that the police laboriously cleared was blocked again as soon as it was seen that Queen Mary was in it. They waved and smiled and cheered and shouted congratulations to the most stately and respected of royal figures, now a great-grandmother for the first time.

At a quarter past midnight a police car nosed slowly in and out, the loud-speaker repeating over and over again: 'Ladies and gentlemen, it is requested from the Palace that we have a little quietness, if you please.' But the message was drowned by the noise of singing. At last the chilly air and the extinguishing of the lights inside the building achieved what the police had not managed. The parked cars that stretched far down the Mall were climbed into, started up and driven away. Enthusiasts who had long missed their last buses and Tube trains began to make their way home on foot. Sir William and Sir John stayed overnight. Mr. Peel and Mr. Hall left at 2 a.m., and by then all was quiet.

Pinned up outside the Home Office in Whitehall and on the door of the Mansion House in the City were notices signed by James Chuter Ede, the first Home Secretary for more than a hundred years to have been absent from the birth of a royal baby with close connexions to the Throne. The custom is of unknown antiquity, but took its final shape after James II's wife, Mary of Modena, was accused of having produced a changeling son as heir to the throne in 1688 —notwithstanding that all the available Privy Councillors were ranged at the foot of the Queen's bed and the Lord Chancellor stood on the step. It had continued right down to the birth of this new baby's mother and aunt. Joynson-Hicks waited downstairs at 17 Bruton Street while Princess Elizabeth was born; four years later J. R. Clynes was called to Glamis too early because of a miscalculation, spent a fortnight waiting at Airlie Castle and then, after a hasty eight-mile dash, learned that Princess Margaret had been born a few minutes before he arrived.

For a long time it was considered necessary for a Minister of the Crown to be actually in the room when the birth took place. When the future Edward VII was born, Sir James Graham waited at one end of an enormous chamber while the young Queen Victoria lay in a heavily curtained four-poster bed at the other. As soon as he had heard the baby cry and had seen him held up by the midwife he made ready to leave, but thought that before he did so he should make some polite remark to his Sovereign. Advancing towards the bed, he said: 'I congratulate Your Majesty most warmly; a very fine boy, if I may say so.' In a faint but indignant voice, the Queen replied from behind the curtains: 'A very fine *Prince*, Sir James.'

It was a custom that had little beyond its age to recommend it, and there was general approval when, in advance of the birth of Princess Elizabeth's child, King George VI issued a formal announcement that 'The attendance of a Minister of the Crown at a birth in the Royal Family is not a statutory requirement or a constitutional necessity. It is merely the survival of an archaic custom, and the King feels it unnecessary to continue further a practice for which there is no legal requirement.'

So Mr. Chuter Ede simply waited by the telephone and then signed the typewritten announcement. Dated November 14, 1948, it said: 'Her Royal Highness the Princess Elizabeth, Duchess of Edinburgh, was safely delivered of a

Prince at 9.14 o'clock this evening. Her Royal Highness and the infant Prince are both well.'

The telegrams that carried the news beyond Britain to the rest of the world had already been prepared, complete except for blank spaces to insert 'Prince' or 'Princess', 'boy' or 'girl'. The baby was a boy. More than a boy—a Prince. And more than a Prince—the first-born son of the King's elder daughter. He was a future King of England.[1]

It is not surprising that within a week after the baby's birth one of the serious Sunday papers was already speculating on the course his education would take. Four years at a preparatory school, three at Eton, then on to the Royal Naval College at Dartmouth: it was not a very revolutionary guess. The baby's cousins, Princes William and Richard of Gloucester, were going to a preparatory school and then, like their father, to Eton before entering the Army; now, with the raising of the entry age at Dartmouth, it would be possible to combine Eton with a career in the Navy.

1. He was 5th in descent from Queen Victoria; 11th from the Electress Sophia, who is the root of title to the Throne under the Act of Settlement; 13th from James I and VI, who united the two Crowns of Great Britain, 32nd from William the Conqueror, tracing through the senior Yorkist line though he was also descended from John of Gaunt, the ancestor of the Lancastrian kings; 39th from Alfred the Great (from which point the Anglo-Saxon chronicles carry the pedigree back in direct male line to the god Woden). He was 14th in descent from Mary, Queen of Scots; 23rd, through her, from Robert the Bruce (or 22nd through the Bowes-Lyons); and 28th from St. Margaret. Through Henry Tudor he was 24th in descent from Llewellyn-ap-Gruffyd, Prince of All Wales. Through his father, the Duke of Edinburgh, he had the blood of Harold II, last of the Anglo-Saxon kings, and was the first male-line descendant of the kings of Denmark in the British royal family since the death of King Harthacnut in 1042. In the remoter regions of the pedigree may be found many of the great names of history and romance: Charlemagne and St. Louis and Frederick the Wonder of the World; Vortigern and Cadwallader; Neill of the Nine Hostages and the High Kings of Erin; even Musa ibn Naseir, an Arab sheikh who was born in Mecca in 660. But one only has to look back six generations—one more than to Queen Victoria though along a different line—to come upon such modest names as George Smith and Mary Browne.

But for most people the immediate interest lay in what the baby's name would be. His birth—and sex—had been celebrated by changing the floodlighting in Trafalgar Square, so that during the following week the fountains played in a delicate shade of blue 'for a boy', and the Poet Laureate had greeted his arrival with four lines of official verse.[1] His title of Prince was already known, though it was not until the week before he was born that the King made certain he would have it.

The need to define the baby's title sprang from the fact that in February 1947, shortly before Philip Mountbatten became engaged to Princess Elizabeth, he surrendered his title of Prince of Greece and Denmark together with all other foreign dignities. On November 19, the day before his marriage, he was dubbed a knight in the Order of the Garter by George VI, granted the style of His Royal Highness, and raised to the peerage as Baron Greenwich, Earl of Merioneth and Duke of Edinburgh. But the King did not specifically grant him the title of Prince.[2] Under the royal warrant

1. A HOPE FOR THE NEWLY BORN (by John Masefield)
    May destiny, allotting what befalls,
      Grant to the newly-born this saving grace,
    A guard more sure than ships and fortress-walls,
      The loyal love and service of a race.

2. The reason for this may be that King George VI supposed the style of Royal Highness carried that of Prince with it. He consistently spoke of his son-in-law as Prince Philip; and the late General Sir Frederick Browning, Comptroller to the Duke of Edinburgh, told me that the King went to his grave still believing that the Duke actually was a Prince. I once ventured to take this point up with a pre-eminent authority, Sir George Bellew, then Garter King of Arms. If, I said, the King, who is the fountain of honour, habitually spoke of 'Prince Philip', surely this description must thereby have acquired some definite standing. It must be something more than a mere nickname, like Lord George Sanger or Duke Ellington; and I suggested that by the King's usage, taken up and followed in the Royal Family and Household, 'Prince' had become the Duke's courtesy title, borne, that is, by social convention and not by legal right. Sir George, however, would have none of this, but under pressure agreed to compromise by calling it a 'courtesy appellation'.

issued by George V in 1917, when he asked members of the Royal Family to give up their German titles and also overhauled the whole system, the title of Prince was limited to the children of a Sovereign and of his sons—not his daughters. If Princess Elizabeth gave birth to a son he would have merely the courtesy use of his father's second title: Earl of Merioneth; and a daughter would be known simply as Lady (Anne or Mary, etc.) Mountbatten.

To set this right, the King, on November 9, 1948, issued letters patent under the Great Seal conferring on all children to be born to the Duke and Duchess of Edinburgh the style of His or Her Royal Highness and the title of Prince or Princess with the Christian name. This put Princess Elizabeth in this respect in the same position as if she had been the Sovereign's son, and at the same time settled a point of precedence that constitutional historians had been disputing for fifty years. Until now it had been seriously argued by a few that, since in English law there is no rule of primogeniture among females and all daughters rank equally in dividing an inheritance, on George VI's death Princess Elizabeth would have no stronger claim to the throne than Princess Margaret.[1] There could now be no question of her superior status.

1. The great genealogist and historian Horace Round raised this question in 1893, concluding that unless Parliament did something about it, we might some day be faced with 'the vacancy of the Throne'. Round's paper went unanswered, but his argument continued to crop up in technical journals in the following half-century. When George VI acceded, with two daughters next in succession, I myself attempted, in an anonymous article, to answer. I succeeded in convincing myself that Princess Elizabeth was the true heir; but the more I studied the subject the more uncertain I felt that all interested parties would agree with me. The situation I thought possible was that at the death of the King some recalcitrant Dominion, say South Africa, might announce that its government accepted Round's view, that the Empire must be divided, and that this Dominion would tender its allegiance, whether she liked it or not, to Queen Margaret II.

A question based on my article was asked in Parliament, and the Home Secretary, Sir John Simon, replied that he was advised that there was no

The baby had already been taken for walks in the grounds of Buckingham Palace in the same perambulator that his mother had used twenty-two years before. The Queen's sister, Countess Granville, told a gathering of Girl Guides in Northern Ireland that 'he could not be more angelic looking. He is golden-haired and has the most beautiful complexion, as well as amazingly delicate features for so young a baby.' But his mother, writing to her former music teacher, Mabel 'Goosey' Lander, and telling her that 'the baby is very sweet and we are enormously proud of him', was more impressed by his hands: 'They are rather large, but fine with long fingers—quite unlike mine and certainly unlike his father's. It will be interesting to see what they will become. I still find it difficult to believe I have a baby of my own!'

On December 15 the baby Prince received his name. The Palace chapel, wrecked by a German dive-bombing attack in September 1940, had not yet been restored, so the Lily Font, made for the baptism of Queen Victoria's first child in 1840, was brought from Windsor and set up in the white and gold Music Room. The font was filled with Jordan water, a custom dating as far back as the Crusades. The baby was dressed in a robe of Honiton lace over satin which had been worn at their christenings by all of Queen Victoria's children, and after them by George VI, his brothers and sisters, his nephews and nieces, the Gloucesters and Kents,

doubt that Princess Elizabeth was the sole heiress. Rather relieved by this downright statement, I asked Simon, whom I happened to meet at dinner the next week, on what reasoning it was based. He answered: 'I haven't studied the matter myself; I went by Donald's advice'—meaning Sir Donald Somervell, the Attorney General, an old friend of us both. Somervell was also of the party that night, so after dinner I repeated my question to him. He answered: 'I have said that Princess Elizabeth is sole heiress; and wild horses won't make me commit myself to reasons.'

There the question rested, to be raised at least once more before 1948 in a New Zealand legal review, by a writer who evidently thought that the British Home Secretary's opinion, unsupported by reasons, carried no weight.

and by his own two daughters, Elizabeth and Margaret. The godparents were the King and Queen; Princess Margaret; the King of Norway; David Bowes-Lyon, brother of the Queen; and three of the Duke of Edinburgh's relations, his grandmother the Dowager Marchioness of Milford Haven, his uncle Prince George of Greece, and his cousin Lady Brabourne. Of these eight only four are still living— Queen Elizabeth the Queen Mother, Princess Margaret, Prince George and Lady Brabourne. The baby was baptized by the Archbishop of Canterbury, assisted by the Dean of the Chapel Royal, and the Prince thus became a member of the Church of England, as by law any wearer of the Crown of the United Kingdom must be.

The name given to the baby was Charles Philip Arthur George. 'Philip' and 'George' came from his father and grandfather. 'Arthur' is the most historic of British royal names, especially in the traditions of the peoples of Celtic blood. Henry VII, the first Welsh King of England, gave it to his eldest son (who died young) in celebration of the ancient people from which he sprang; but more recently the name had come back into the Royal Family at the christening of Queen Victoria's third son, whose godfather was the aged Arthur, Duke of Wellington; and this Prince Arthur, afterwards Duke of Connaught, had survived to be a godfather of Princess Elizabeth herself.

The name 'Charles' came as a surprise: it had not been borne by a reigning sovereign since the death of Charles II in 1685. Two years later, when Princess Anne was christened, people began to suppose that this was a conscious attempt to revive the royal Stuart names. But the parents have since let it be known that no such idea occurred to them. Their eldest son might be taken to be named after one of his godfathers, who had been Prince Charles of Denmark before changing his name to Haakon on accession to the throne of Norway. But even this would be an afterthought.

[9]

Princess Elizabeth and the Duke called their children Charles and Anne for no more subtle reason than that these are the boy's and girl's names they happen to like best. Princess Margaret, on the other hand, was reported to have said: 'Oh dear! I suppose now they'll call me Charley's Aunt!'

The christening party that followed was held in the White Drawing Room, in the north-west corner of the State Apartments, the windows looking out over the garden; but the celebratory cake-cutting and renewed congratulations were overhung with a hint of sadness. Although the King had been able to attend the christening, his health was giving great anxiety. His doctors had advised him not to undertake the tour that would have carried him right round the world to Australia, New Zealand and Canada. The announcement had been delayed until two days after Prince Charles's birth for fear of upsetting Princess Elizabeth.[1] But she knew that the King had been in bad health for some time and, though the doctors hoped that his condition would respond to treatment, he was not fit enough to make even the journey to Sandringham. For the first time for many years the Royal Family celebrated Christmas at Buckingham Palace.

Charles had spent the first month of his life in the dressing room adjoining his mother's bedroom. The round wicker basket in which he slept had, like his christening robe, been handed down through the family since Queen Victoria's times. His hairbrush and silver rattle had, like his perambulator, been used by his mother when she was a child. The familiar objects were imbued with a sense of continuity—only the faces changed. Sister Helen Rowe withdrew and was replaced by two Scottish-born nurses, Helen Lightbody

1. The secret was very closely guarded. The night before the announcement I attended a sherry party at Buckingham Palace with other press correspondents to meet the members of the Household who should have been in attendance but who now knew, of course, that the tour would not take place. Though its prospects were naturally much discussed, the guests dispersed with no inkling of the announcement immediately to come.

and Mabel Anderson. Miss Lightbody—always given the courtesy title of 'Mrs.', since she was the senior of the two—had brought up the Duke of Gloucester's children and was already known to Princess Elizabeth. Miss Anderson, still in her early twenties, had been working for six years since she left her training school. With her current job shortly coming to an end, she had put an advertisement in the 'Situations Wanted' columns of a nurse's magazine, and was very pleasantly surprised when she was asked to call at Buckingham Palace and found herself being interviewed by Princess Elizabeth. There were several other nurses in the running, but the Princess's choice fell on her—and the employment turned out to be steady. She stayed on at the Palace to look after Princess Anne, and then Andrew, and now she is in charge of Edward as well.

Before Charles's birth, the Edinburghs had lived in a rented house at Windlesham, whose lease was now expiring. The fact that Buckingham Palace has upwards of six hundred rooms did not make them any less anxious than other young married couples to get out of their parents' home and into an establishment of their own, but Clarence House, where the King had planned to settle them as soon as they were married, was taking a great time to be set into shape. Once the home of the Duke of Clarence who became William IV, it had been lent by the King to the British Red Cross Society during the war and converted into very severe sets of offices. Even before that, the house had been derelict since the first Duke of Connaught retired to live at Bagshot soon after the first world war. It needed restoring and converting as well as redecorating and, with a great scarcity of men and materials in the building trade so soon after the end of the war, the work took over a year. It was not until July 1949 that the Princess and the Duke were able to move into their new home, transformed from a rambling mansion that had been old-fashioned even in Victorian times, without bathrooms or electric light, into a modern, efficient, dignified and attractive town house.

It was a big cube of solid masonry, the back facing York House, where the last Prince of Wales had lived (and was succeeded by his brother, the Duke of Gloucester), and the front looking across its own square garden to the Mall and St. James's Park. The garden, entered by an inconspicuous door at the side, was walled and invisible from street level. Whenever the Princess was in residence her banner—the royal arms differenced by a silver label (that is, a white band across the top with three pendants) charged with a red rose between two crosses of St. George—flew from the flagstaff on the roof. And just below the flag, with windows looking out over the garden and the park, were the nursery quarters, chintz-curtained, decorated in pale blue. In the day nursery, which was also the nurses' sitting room, the small Prince learned to crawl around the table in the centre of the room, past the two low armchairs beside it and the bigger pair that stood on each side of the mesh-protected fireplace, and back to the sofa and the glass-fronted case where toys and picture books were kept, before being lifted into his folding playpen.

Two nurserymaids kept the quarters tidy; a nursery foot-man brought food (the nursery kitchen was not installed until after Princess Anne's birth a year later) and kept contact with the rest of the household. Every day Mrs. Light-body or Miss Anderson would take Charles for a walk round the garden in his perambulator, or even risk recognition in St. James's Park or Green Park—though, since they always wore ordinary nursing uniform, with nothing to distinguish them from the other nannies out for a stroll in the park, it was not usual for them to be forced to make a hasty retreat to the protection of the walled garden and the sentry at the gate.

The Prince of Wales's earliest memory is of that perambulator, not of its softness or bounciness or even the people who tried to peep in, but of its prodigious length, from where he sat to where hands were pushing at the other end. In it, besides going to the park, he would sometimes be wheeled to neighbouring Marlborough House, to visit Queen Mary, whom he called 'Gan-Gan', the same nickname that the last Prince of Wales, now Duke of Windsor, used for Queen Victoria. Charles was less than four and a half years old when Queen Mary died, yet he still retains a vivid memory of her, sitting very upright with her feet resting on a footstool, surrounded by enormous cabinets of jade objects, part of the famous collection of precious things that she built up over her long lifetime. When the Queen and Princess Margaret were that age, they were never allowed to touch a thing, but the old lady let Charles meddle with anything he liked. The child brought a ray of sunshine into a life that towards the end was increasingly clouded by sadness. Queen Mary lived to see her husband and three of her sons die, and another go into exile; on this small boy she fixed her hopes for the future of the dynasty that she had done so much to hold high in the world's esteem.

The King's health had not improved. In March 1949 he underwent another operation, more serious and, in what it revealed, most alarming. He realized now, as did all the Royal Family, that he had not long to live. With characteristic determination he went quietly about as many duties as he could perform; the regular royal round was resumed: Balmoral in the late summer, Sandringham at Christmas, Windsor at Easter and weekends. In August 1950 he was delighted by the birth of a grand-daughter, Princess Anne, and that Christmas he and the Queen looked after the two children while Princess Elizabeth went off to Malta to spend the holiday with her husband, still a serving officer in the Royal Navy. (The Duke of Edinburgh had been gazetted a Lieutenant-Commander on the day Anne was born, and now had his own ship, the frigate *Magpie*.) 'Charles is too sweet, stumping around the room,' the King wrote to the Princess. 'We shall love having him at Sandringham. He is the fifth generation to live there and I hope he will get to love the place.'

Their father was at sea; and their mother was now increasingly called upon to fulfil royal engagements that the King was too ill to perform. Yet Miss Anderson, looking back on Charles's early childhood, is convinced that he and Anne saw more of their parents than most children in homes where nurses are employed. It is not surprising that in a family where the father, grandfather and great-grandfather —two kings and a royal consort—all served as naval officers the daily timetable was worked out with remarkable precision. And despite the official duties which absorbed so much of the time of the Princess and the Duke, both parents were determined to devote every possible moment of their free time to the children. Consequently certain times of the day were irrevocably set aside for their mother. The first was after breakfast, from nine to nine-thirty, when Mrs. Lightbody took the children down to play with her; another was after tea, when the Princess went up to the nursery for an hour and a half, romping with the children on the nursery floor, bathing them and finally tucking them up in bed. If she could snatch other moments during the day to be with them she did so, but nothing was ever allowed to encroach on these morning and evening playtimes so long as she was in London.

The children were got up (they seldom needed waking) at seven, washed, dressed and given their breakfast. They played in the nursery until their nine o'clock visit to Mummy, and when they were brought upstairs again it was time to be dressed for the morning walk, from ten-thirty to noon. Miss Anderson or Mrs. Lightbody pushed the pram and a plain-clothes constable followed at what had to be a carefully calculated interval, not too far away to be able to give protection, not too close to become conspicuous. Acting as rather more aggressive bodyguards were the two corgis, the breed of dogs that have become as closely identi- fied with the present Royal Family as spaniels were with the Stuarts. At that time they were Susan and Sugar; today you can still trip over their staid and slightly torpid successors on the nursery floor at Buckingham Palace: Prince Charles's Whisky and Princess Anne's Sherry.

Back in the nursery, luncheon was at one o'clock: consumed as far as Charles was concerned with a truly royal appetite, his particular preference at this time being for boiled chicken and rice. After lunch came the compulsory rest until three- thirty and then a spell in the garden or a visit to Queen Mary at Marlborough House or the Queen at Buckingham Palace, returning for tea at four-thirty and games with their mother.

In spite of all the efforts the nurses made to avoid recogni- tion, there were times when the regular appearances of the little group in the parks adjoining Clarence House began to be anticipated and crowds would follow them along the gravel walks. When this became oppressive the children were taken by car to the comparative seclusion of Richmond Park or Wimbledon Common, wilder and less frequented than St. James's or the Green Park. Here there was more room for practice in the new art of walking upright, with help from Jumbo, a blue elephant on wheels, which the un- certain pedestrian could half lean on and half push. Jumbo remained Prince Charles's favourite toy for years, and is still in the nursery at Buckingham Palace, faded, rather grubby, and tuskless, but as popular with the younger princes as he was with his first owner. Later on, as Charles's footsteps grew more confident, there were games of hide-and-seek in the Richmond bracken, and football matches in which the chauffeur and the detective helped to make up the sides.

The demands on their parents' time grew heavier and the shadow cast over the Royal Family by anxiety about the

King's health grew longer. In July 1951 the Duke gave up his command of the *Magpie*, and in October, their departure delayed for two weeks by a new operation on the King, the Duke and the Princess flew to Montreal for a tour that took them across Canada from the Atlantic to the Pacific and over the border for a brief visit to Washington. With her the Princess carried a sealed envelope containing the formal documents that she would have to sign if her father died and she was called to the Throne. She and her mother had been told—though the King himself did not know—that he was suffering from cancer. But happily he was still alive when they returned for Christmas at Sandringham, hollow-cheeked and grey from long illness, but delighting in the company of his three-year-old grandson and year-old grand-daughter.

It is from this period that the Prince of Wales today recalls his only memory of his grandfather: the impression of sitting on a sofa with somebody much bigger than himself while another figure (it was in fact Richard Colville, the Press Secretary) swung something shiny on the end of his watch chain, trying to hold his attention and keep him still. It was November 14, Charles's third birthday, and the photograph that was being taken was ready for his parents on their return. The framed picture stands in the Queen's private sitting room: especially dear to her because it combines almost her last memory of her father with one of the earliest portraits of her son. By Her Majesty's permission it is reproduced opposite p. 34.

On January 30, 1952, the King was well enough to take his daughter and son-in-law to *South Pacific* at Drury Lane—the first time he had visited a theatre for many months. The next day he stood haggard and lonely, at London Airport, his frail body seeming almost too weak to withstand the breeze that blew across the tarmac, waving to them as they set off on the great Commonwealth tour that he had had to postpone at the time of Charles's birth and had never since had the strength to undertake.

The picture of this pale, courageous man, broadcast through television and newspapers, brought a wave of sadness to millions of families throughout Britain and the Commonwealth. Yet the suddenness of his death less than a week later still came as a tremendous shock. After a day's shooting at Sandringham he went to bed on February 5 and failed to wake in the morning. He had died in his sleep some time in the early hours of February 6. The news of his death was announced at a quarter to eleven that morning and the chilly grey mist that shrouded Sandringham all day seemed to drift out and embrace the whole country.

The white blinds were drawn over the windows of Buckingham Palace. At St. Paul's a bell began to toll at 11.50 and continued every minute for the next two hours. Shop displays were removed and the windows draped in black. Parliament met and the sittings of both Houses were suspended until the evening. On the other side of Bridge Street a newspaper placard had fallen on the ground, face upward. 'The King is Dead', it said. The passengers bustling in and out of Westminster Underground station suddenly split into two streams as they came to it, careful not to tread on it yet saying nothing, unwilling to make a show of their respect.

At five o'clock the Accession Council, meeting at St. James's Palace, declared Princess Elizabeth to be the new Sovereign, and at seven the Lords and Commons began to take the oath of allegiance.

At the hunting lodge on the Sagana River that the people of Kenya had given her as a wedding present Princess Elizabeth was resting after a night spent at Treetops, a little cabin perched in a huge fig-tree overlooking a water hole— a famous place for observing the game that abounded in the Aberdare Mountains—and a morning fishing in the river. The telephone rang at the lodge, the call was taken by

Michael Parker—it was the Princess's Private Secretary, Martin Charteris, speaking from the Outspan Hotel on the other side of the valley. A reporter from the *East African Standard* had just told him that his paper had received the news that the King was dead. Parker tried to confirm this by telephoning Nairobi, but the Governor had already left on his way to meet the Princess at her next stop, Mombasa. Other newspapers were now informing the Royal Tour reporters of the news. Parker could not get the B.B.C. bulletins, but the sound of solemn music seemed sufficient confirmation. He drew the Duke of Edinburgh from the long sitting room at the lodge without attracting the Princess's attention. The Duke went back and broke the news to her. The time was 2.45 p.m.; 11.45 a.m. in London.

She sat at the desk in the sitting room and began her work as Queen. First the telegrams to the governments of the Commonwealth countries that she could not now visit. Authority for the Privy Council to meet as soon as the Accession Council (a larger body) had declared her Queen. The decision on what name she wished to be known by—for she could equally well choose to be Queen Mary or Queen Alexandra as Queen Elizabeth. And while she worked, and for the first time signed herself 'Elizabeth R.', the Duke planned the quickest way to get them back to London.

She had no mourning clothes and for the first part of the journey wore a gaily-patterned beige dress, with a white hat and gloves. The African servants gathered sadly at the door and her chauffeur knelt to kiss her shoes. They drove to Nanyuki airfield, on the equator, where the welcoming flags were still flying, and from there flew to Entebbe. For three hours they waited until a tropical storm had blown itself out; then the aircraft that had brought them from London Airport a week before took off on the sad homeward journey. At six minutes past four on the afternoon of February 7 the Argonaut *Atalanta* had descended from

16,500 feet to 4,000 feet and was above Sevenoaks, heading along Amber Airways 2 and due at London Airport at 4.19. At 4.30 it taxied to a halt at the spot where the Duke of Gloucester, the Prime Minister (Winston Churchill) and other members of the Cabinet were waiting bareheaded to receive their new Sovereign.

The crowds along the Mall were silent. Queen Mary, still erect, stood waiting at the porch of Clarence House to greet them. As the car stopped, the Royal Banner was run up on the flagstaff.

Next morning at St. James's Palace, at Charing Cross beneath the statue of Charles I, at Temple Bar, on the steps of the Royal Exchange, in Edinburgh at the Mercat Cross, the accession of the new Queen was proclaimed by Garter King of Arms, by Lancaster Herald, by Norroy and Ulster King of Arms, by Clarenceux King of Arms, by the Provost and the Lord Lyon King of Arms.

. . . 'We do now hereby with one voice and Consent of Tongue and Heart publish and proclaim that the High and Mighty Princess Elizabeth Alexandra Mary is now, by the Death of our late Sovereign of Happy Memory, become Queen Elizabeth the Second, by the Grace of God Queen of this Realm and of all Her other Realms and Territories, Head of the Commonwealth, Defender of the Faith, to whom her lieges do acknowledge all Faith and constant Obedience, with hearty and humble Affection; beseeching God, by whom Kings and Queens do reign, to bless the Royal Princess Elizabeth the Second with long and happy Years to reign over us.'

In Friary Court, just up the road from Clarence House, Garter finished reading and raised his cocked hat. The black-draped regimental standard was lowered and the band, for the first time in fifty-one years, played 'God Save the Queen'. From Hyde Park came the thud at ten-second intervals of the forty-one-gun salute. The mourning flags were raised to the tops of their masts for the rest of the day.

## { 2 }

# CHARLES, DUKE OF CORNWALL

THE Queen's accession made no immediate change in her children's lives. Prince Charles's education, though much discussed, could not yet progress beyond playing with alphabet blocks in the nursery sessions with Mummy. He was still too young to appreciate the antiquity of his new title as Duke of Cornwall[1] or to make use of the argument that, as Heir Apparent, he had now legally come of age.[2] He still lived at Clarence House, though with a different

1. The earldom dates from 1140. Richard, King of the Romans, younger brother of Henry III, was the first royal earl. After the death of his son Edmund, without heirs, the dignity was given by Edward II to his hated favourite, Piers Gaveston. Gaveston was lynched on Blacklow Hill in 1312 and the earldom reverted to the Crown. Edward III gave it to his younger brother, Lord John of Eltham, who died young and childless and lies under one of the loveliest monuments in Westminster Abbey. In 1337 Edward III introduced into England the new title of Duke (which he himself had borne in Aquitaine) and granted the dukedom of Cornwall to his eldest son, Edward of Woodstock (in later centuries called the Black Prince) and 'the eldest sons of his heirs being Kings of England'. This charter is still in force, and is deemed to operate in favour of the eldest son of the reigning King or Queen, notwithstanding that no Sovereign since 1688 has been the heir of the Black Prince.

2. This theory was propounded by the legal antiquary, the late Edward Iwi, in 1966. It has not, as yet, been adopted by any established authority.

flag on the roof. Granny and Aunt Margot were still at Buckingham Palace, Gan-Gan still at Marlborough House, and Mummy exactly the same when she came to bath him and Anne and put them to bed.[1]

If anything, the Princess's transformation into Queen had brought slightly less, rather than more, ceremony into the children's lives. For example, Charles had been taught always to bow at the door when he entered a room where his grandparents, the King and Queen, were sitting. His grandmother—now to be known as Queen Elizabeth the Queen Mother[2]—always impressed upon the King the necessity for him to preserve a certain degree of aloofness, though all his natural inclinations were against it and he sometimes remembered with regret the easy intimacy that he had enjoyed at his boys' camps and other activities when he was Duke of York. When he came to the Throne, Queen Elizabeth insisted that the unbending must be left to her, and that the crowned and anointed King must not be too ready to step down from his pedestal—and that even in the nursery some touches of majesty were not out of place: an argument that had the full approval of Queen Mary. But the new Queen and her husband could not bear to put even this slight barrier between their children and themselves: instructions were given that Charles and Anne were not to bow and curtsey to them, though they should continue to do so when they went to Marlborough House. Although this was known only within the domestic circle of Clarence

1. Making light of my estimate of the Queen's domestic preoccupations, Mr. Kingsley Martin, in *The Crown and the Establishment*, writes: 'Mr. Morrah does not pretend that she baths the baby or cooks the meals.' She does not cook the meals, except perhaps on an occasional picnic at Balmoral. But she seldom missed a chance to bath the baby. It was not necessary to mention this in a book called *The Work of the Queen*, for she did not regard bathing her babies as work. What young mother does?

2. In the Royal Household Queen Elizabeth II is usually referred to as the Queen and her mother as Queen Elizabeth. Except where another sense is obvious from the context I follow the same practice from now on.

House at that time, it was the first sign of the change of tone that was to mark the new reign. As time went by, more and more people became aware that the old ceremony and protocol were to be softened down.

The children were much too young to attend their grand-father's funeral, and had in fact remained at Sandringham, to avoid the possibility of their seeing, from the nursery windows of Clarence House, the majestic, mournful procession as the coffin was escorted along the Mall on its way to burial in St. George's Chapel at Windsor. But the old habit of spending Easter at Windsor was observed, a muted holiday with the Court still in mourning, and on their return they found they had a new home. Queen Elizabeth and Princess Margaret had moved to Clarence House. The Queen and the Duke of Edinburgh had taken up residence in the first- and second-floor apartments on the north side of the quadrangle, and the nursery was now installed in the top storey above them.

The half-dozen rooms looking out over Constitution Hill —one of them, at the corner, commanding a view of the Palace forecourt, where the guard is changed—had been redecorated in the same style as the nurseries they had left with a predominant shade of pale blue. Younger children having been added to the family, they are nurseries still, and still familiar ground to Prince Charles, who enjoys playing the part of big brother in his juniors' games. They remain today very much what they were in his childhood, or what they became soon after his arrival, when lessons began and one of them was fitted up as a schoolroom. Neither this room nor the big day nursery next door is ostentatiously functional. They are furnished in the main with simple and comfortable chintz-covered chairs and sofas, suitable for adult visitors or the nursery staff, together with one or two miniature tables and chairs for the children. In the night nurseries Mrs. Lightbody had the baby Princess to sleep with her, while Miss Anderson looked after Prince Charles at night. After a little time a small kitchen was fitted up in the nursery suite; but in the earlier days meals were brought up by the nursery page from the main Palace kitchen and kept warm on hot-plates—which are still there and sometimes used for the younger princes' breakfast.

The litter of toys on the nursery floor included picture books, toy soldiers, bricks, pencils, crayons and paints. There were teddy bears and other woolly animals and Charles's favourite bear, which eventually accompanied him to school. One noticeable feature differentiated this nursery from most. Toy motor cars and aircraft, though they do exist, were almost all out of sight. All down the corridor outside the nursery were parked those vehicles which were too big to be brought into the room. They were all horse-drawn. Prince Charles had his tricycle, which he rode at great speed round Richmond Park. But he was not and is not, by the standards of most of his contemporaries, mechanically minded. Princess Anne, when she was a little older, grew to be the more passionately interested of the two in horses, taking after her mother. But recently Charles has caught his father's enthusiasm for polo, and from his earliest days he has preferred animals to machines.

By the time the family moved into their new home Prince Charles was three and a half. He was now very much a person, with a distinguishable character of his own. The Queen, looking back on the infancy of all her four children, is clear that even before Prince Edward could walk they were all quite different from one another.

Others, with no doubt a less penetrating eye for idiosyncrasy than a mother's, have suggested resemblances. Colonel Miller, the Crown Equerry, who began to know the Prince only when he was asked to help teach him to ride, thinks he took after his grandmother, Queen Elizabeth. Miss Anderson thinks he was always uniquely himself; that Princess

Anne is like her father (in character, not appearance); Prince
Andrew is a mixture of the two elder children, and Prince
Edward is a mixture of Princess Anne and Prince Andrew.

This shrewd and interesting characterization, however,
leaves as an unknown quantity, so far, the temperament of
Prince Charles himself. Everybody who remembers his
childhood agrees that he was an exceptionally sweet-
natured little boy. They also speak of his thoughtfulness, in
both connotations of the word. He was thoughtful to others
and thoughtful about the world around him. He looks in his
early photograph rather a solemn child; but this belies his
character, for he quickly developed a bubbling sense of
humour. The apparent seriousness in the photographs may
probably be accounted for in another way: he suffered a
good deal from shyness, which indeed he has not even now
entirely overcome. In this respect he is in direct contrast
with his grandmother, Queen Elizabeth, whom Colonel
Miller thinks he particularly resembles, for she is the most
obviously expansive or 'extrovert' member of the Royal
Family.

In Prince Charles there was always a hint of restraint,
withdrawal—the opposite of his sister's easy, outgoing
manner. Whenever they travelled by car and the crowds
recognized and greeted them it was always Anne who
replied with waves of the hand, carefully copied from her
mother. Charles was for a long time too bashful to do the
same.

This was certainly not due to any precocious sense of
position, of being different from other children, any awareness that there are some little boys and girls around whom
crowds do not gather to wave and to be waved at. The
Queen, looking back on her own childhood, cannot fix on
any particular incident when this awareness came to her; nor
did she ever notice any moment of sudden enlightenment in
her son. All through his nursery days everybody, high or

low, spoke to him simply as Charles. He knew from an early age that he had a longer name, 'Prince Charles', which people used when they were talking *about* him—but all his friends had longer names too: Master Tommy, Miss Betty or Lady Jane. Miss Anderson, who saw more of him than did anybody else, never noticed any sign that he was conscious of a difference between his friends' names and his own. It was his mother's wish that nobody should be in a hurry to enlighten him.

He took his environment for granted, and seemed even to hold aloof from it. There were the scarlet-coated sentries at the door, for instance, with tall bearskins, and bayonets fixed to their rifles, and a habit of going through a complicated, clattering series of motions when certain people went by. A generation before, Charles's mother had discovered that she was one of the persons who could set off this intriguing machinery of presenting arms, just by walking in front of the sentry; and, having discovered it, she could not resist the temptation of strolling backwards and forwards to have it repeated over and over again. Anne, when she had learned to walk, made the same discovery and, whenever opportunity permitted, played the same game. But Charles never did. He liked playing with tin soldiers in the nursery. He admired the real soldiers in the courtyard and imitated their drill. But he never went beyond watching them, waiting to see what they would do, not asserting his own power and privilege of making them do it. In contrast to the hint of imperiousness in his sister, his own dominant trait in dealing with other people was a precocious consideration, a reluctance to put them to unnecessary trouble.

As they developed it became clear that Charles was the more biddable of the two. He was far from being a goody-goody child and could lose his temper with the best, but his outbursts of rage, like those of his grandfather George VI, were sudden squalls, quickly over. Like any other brother,

he squabbled from time to time with his sister, once she
had reached an age to stand up for herself and show that she
had a will of her own. But when these little tiffs had blown
over it was always Charles who was the first to say he was
sorry.

When he deserved it he was spanked. The occasion did not
often arise. One point on which parental discipline was
sternly enforced was that the children should never be rude
to others (since the 'others', whether children or adult, were
not in a position to answer back). Charles's father once
caught him making faces at people and he was promptly
punished, and when he was older the Queen had to rebuke
him for omitting 'Mr.' when he spoke to a senior detective,
but these were the sort of faults that he was least likely to
commit, with his almost supersensitive awareness of other
people's feelings. If he did get spanked or slapped he soon
forgot it, certainly not regarding it as an affront to his
princely dignity. Later, when he got into trouble at
Gordonstoun and lost some privileges, he admitted that he
would have much preferred to be caned and get it over.
Mrs. Lightbody and Miss Anderson received letters
from time to time urging that the future monarch should
not be exposed to corporal punishment—just as the Queen
received a steady stream of advice on the lines his education
should take—and all these were answered by a lady-in-
waiting, sometimes by the Queen herself. But the nurses,
having learned by experience that such punishments as
sending Charles to his room in disgrace were less effective
and more deeply resented, continued to enforce discipline
in the old-fashioned way.

His concern for good manners, whether inbred or impressed on him by Mrs. Lightbody and Miss Anderson, led
him to take a hand in his small sister's education. At the end
of a railway journey he would without prompting lead her
up the platform to say thank you to the driver. It was be-

cause of enthusiasm as well as seniority that he set her an example in other courtesies. But she could be stubborn, and not always led. When they went to Marlborough House with a birthday bunch of flowers for Gan-Gan, Charles halted at the door and gravely bowed, but he found it quite impossible to persuade Anne to curtsey.

As the first year at Buckingham Palace neared its end, Prince Charles was able to give the most ambitious birthday party he had yet enjoyed. On November 14 he was four years old. Fourteen other children were invited to celebrate with him in the white and gold Music Room where his christening party had been held. The corridor outside was cleared of its array of marble busts, chairs and tables and put at the guests' disposal for games and races, while in the forecourt the band of the Grenadier Guards, after playing a succession of nursery rhymes, broke into the host's favourite tune—'The Teddy Bears' Picnic'. It was the lightesthearted party given in Buckingham Palace since the period of the Crimean War, when Queen Victoria still had children young enough to romp in the same spirit.

Two days later Prince Charles made his first appearance at a public entertainment. His mother and grandmother took him to Sir Robert Mayer's concert for children at the Royal Festival Hall. He showed a lively interest, firing questions at Queen Elizabeth about the various instruments that were being played. It was perhaps the first inkling of the taste for music which he has since shown and cultivated. Unfortunately there seems to have been something of the critic in him, too. Halfway through the concert his boredom became too apparent and he had to be taken home.

That Christmas, the first of the new reign, was spent at Sandringham with the whole family present, from Queen Mary to Princess Anne. Gan-Gan was the first to leave, and Charles was allowed to go down to Wolferton station to 'flag' the train away. This is his last clear memory of his great-grandmother, as she stepped into her carriage, and he waved the flag that the stationmaster had given him, blew the whistle and watched the train slowly gather speed. In March Queen Mary died.

★　　　★　　　★

The Coronation had been set for June 2. Ever since the Queen's accession experts of Church and State had been conferring over the details of the ritual and the accompanying ceremonials. It is an essential feature of the Coronation that before the Archbishop consents to crown the Sovereign he obtains from her an oath to protect the Church and maintain the laws and liberties of her subjects; and after the Queen is crowned and enthroned the lords of Church and State swear an oath to her in return—the bishops doing fealty and the peers homage, each swearing to become her liege man 'of life and limb and of earthly worship'. Formerly each in turn knelt at the foot of the throne to take the oath; but nowadays, with the enormously swollen ranks of the peerage, only the royal dukes and the head of each grade— duke, marquess, earl, viscount or baron—make the full gesture, while his juniors kneel in their places and repeat the words with him. This procedure was to be followed; but the first royal duke and the head of the whole peerage is the Duke of Cornwall, and in 1953 he was a little boy four years old.

There was no guidance to be had from precedent; for no Sovereign since the dukedom was created by the charter of 1337 had come to be crowned having a son so young as this. Probably Prince Charles, who enjoyed dressing up and has since shown a great deal of talent as an actor, would have been more than willing to be fitted out with the imposing crimson velvet mantle and ermine cape of a duke, and the coronet of a Queen's son, adorned with alternate fleurs-de-lys and crosses paty, to be donned in the Abbey at the moment when the Archbishop placed the Crown on the Queen's head. Such a coronet had been charmingly worn at the previous Coronation by the six-year-old Princess Margaret, who, it is said, had thrown herself kicking on the nursery floor and refused to budge until she was also promised a velvet train as long as her big sister's. But Princess Margaret had not taken any active part, for girls do not pay homage. Moreover, Prince Charles was two years younger than even his aunt had been when George VI was crowned; and the experience of Sir Robert Mayer's concert warned his parents that his patience as a spectator was by no means inexhaustible. The Queen decided to take the risk that her son, without the oath of allegiance, might develop into a leader of revolt. He should come to the Coronation, but not in ducal robes, nor to sit in a chair of state alongside the other three royal dukes, his father and his great-uncle of Gloucester and his cousin of Kent. He should be brought informally into the royal box over the tomb of Anne of Cleves, where his grandmother and his aunt would sit, and stay for as much of the long ceremony as they judged he could take. Princess Anne was not yet three and would have to stay at home.

For both children the elaborate preparations for the great event provided much of the spice of life in the early months of 1953. They watched the seamstresses at work on the two great velvet trains their mother was to wear on the day—the crimson Parliament Robe in which she would enter the Abbey and the purple Coronation Robe in which she would leave. There was much coming and going of the great. Winston Churchill was often there, leaving Prince Charles the memory of a large man, a large hat and a huge cigar. From the nursery windows or on their walks in the park the children watched the workmen transforming the Mall into an avenue between two continuous grandstands; and upstairs at home the game of 'Coronations' gave splendid opportunities for dressing up as King and Queen, with any-one who could be roped in to play Archbishop, Earl Marshal, Lord Great Chamberlain. Anne, peeping out of the one window that overlooked the forecourt, caught a glimpse of soldiers marching and bands playing, and announced that the Coronation had begun, but was patronizingly informed by Charles that it was only the changing of the guard. So the bustle continued and the colours dazzlingly merged into each other, and in their spare moments the Queen and Queen Elizabeth did their best to bring within childish comprehension what all the growing excitement was about.

When the day came they were up early, wakened by the sound of trumpets and bugles and the stir of the multitudes stretching as far as they could see along the processional way. They watched the mile-long cavalcade passing the statue of Queen Victoria and moving slowly towards the Admiralty Arch; and as the climax they saw their mother and father, in the famous glass coach of George III, attended by posti-lions, footmen and outriders in the full-dress liveries of the Household, drive from the Grand Entrance. As the coach passed through the cheering crowds on its way to the Abbey, Mrs. Lightbody dressed Charles in a white silk suit and took him down to a side door, where they got into a plain car and drove by a roundabout route to Dean's Yard and the Cloisters and so into the Abbey. The Prince's name was not mentioned in the elaborate printed order of ceremonial; and when the small white figure slipped into the front row of the royal box, between his grandmother and Princess Margaret, very few of the people who had a clear view of that side of the sanctuary—they were chiefly the bishops and the peeresses—even noticed that he was there.

He had arrived at the most solemn and sacramental moment of the service. The choir was singing Handel's joyous setting of the anthem 'Zadok the Priest', which has stood in the coronation order (at first in the Latin version

'Unxerunt Salomonem') without a break since King Edgar the Peaceful was crowned at Bath in 973. The Queen had been stripped of her splendid crimson robes and now, in the plainest possible white garment with no jewels save her earrings, was taking her seat in the Coronation Chair, while four Knights of the Garter, in the contrasting magnificence of their blue velvet mantles, held over her a canopy of cloth of gold. It was the moment when she was to be raised to the sanctified rank of queenhood by the anointing with consecrated oil. It is possible that the young Duke of Cornwall was the first heir to the Throne who ever saw this mystical rite performed. For the tradition had been that, because of the mysterious sacredness of the unction, the canopy was held so low that the Sovereign and the Archbishop were alone in a sort of tent, and that the Archbishop pronounced the words of anointing, 'with holy oil, as kings, priests and prophets were anointed', in a hushed voice that none could overhear. But this time tradition was set aside. The canopy was held high; the Archbishop spoke the solemn words aloud; and the Queen, raising her head which she had bowed to receive the unction, glanced to the right and caught the eye of her little son. A smile of affection and understanding seemed to be exchanged between them.

At that moment some of those who were watching the royal box saw Charles pass his hand slowly over his hair. The more romantic wondered if he were imagining himself in his mother's place, or if perhaps somebody had told him of the first Queen Elizabeth's whisper to the bishop who consecrated her, 'This grease stinketh ill'; or even if he was already casting his thoughts forward to the day when he, too, would be consecrated. In fact, having rubbed his hand on his hair, he held it out for his grandmother to smell— Mrs. Lightbody, in honour of the occasion, had given him a new sort of hair-oil.

He kept up a running fire of questions to Queen Elizabeth

and Princess Margaret, but simply because there was so much to ask about, such constant changing of bright uniforms and costumes, prayers and anthems and hymns, he can today scarcely remember a single thing about the ceremony inside the Abbey. It might have been constitutionally improper for him to remain during the act of homage without doing homage himself, and there was in any case a limit to the amount of spectacle that a four-year-old could endure before the fidgets set in, so Mrs. Lightbody took him out through a side door and home to luncheon, while the ritual was completed and the Queen set out on the processional drive through the West End of London to show herself to the thousands who had been unable to get places on the outward route to the Abbey. When she at last got back to the Palace she went out on to the balcony to acknowledge the cheers, still wearing her robes and Crown. She stood alone for a moment, and then the Duke of Edinburgh led the children out by the hand to join her.

This was the first time that Charles had been exposed to one of these great popular royal occasions, the tight-packed masses of people beyond the railings, the uplifted faces, the agitated arms and hats and newspapers, the deafening noise, the bursts of cheering that came in solid waves, the friendliness and wellwishing that kept swelling into deep emotion; his mother beside him robed like a picture-book Queen; scarlet-coated foot guards and steel-cuirassed cavalrymen still marching and wheeling below. This was the panoply, the splendour and the almost frightening enthusiasm that he would one day grow up to inherit. There is a story that he said: 'There won't be another coronation for a long time, and that will be mine.' It isn't in character, and he himself has no recollection of saying anything of the kind. But no child could have lived through these moments without passing a little farther along the path to awareness that he was not like other children.

\*       \*       \*

In November he would be five, the age at which compulsory education begins for every English child. The Queen
had long made up her mind that her children should be
brought up in as like a way as possible to other people's
—though she was not yet ready to take the revolutionary
step of sending them to the primary school round the corner.
One of the rooms in the nursery suite was fitted out with a
small desk and blackboard—and Mispy was brought in.

'Mispy' (Miss P.), as Charles and the Queen's other
children still call her, was a young Glasgow-born woman,
Catherine Peebles, who had been governess to Charles's
cousin, Prince Michael of Kent, until a short time before,
when he went off to school. Princess Marina recommended
her to the Queen and, like Miss Anderson, she has remained
at the Palace ever since, undertaking the early education of
Anne and later Andrew, and no doubt Edward when the
time comes. She is small, dark-haired, humorous and
shrewd. She found that her pupil was sensible and well
behaved, self-contained and with a responsibility beyond
his years. These are the qualities with which he impressed all
those who met him at that time: 'he liked being amused,
rather than amusing himself . . . He was very responsive to
kindness, but if you shouted at him he would draw back
into his shell and for a time you would be able to do nothing with him.' He had a great sense of fun, but it was an
inward amusement not a boisterous cheerfulness, a chuckle
at something that struck him as odd. Now that he has
grown out of a great deal of his shyness and gets a lot of
pleasure out of amateur theatricals, he has a hankering to
play comedy. And it is perhaps significant that the 'Goon'
type of humour appeals most to him.

But in those days he was far too bashful to do any play-acting in public. His dominant passions were still for boiled chicken and rice, and the pet animals that were turning the nursery into a miniature menagerie. The two corgis had been joined by a hamster named Chi-Chi, and Queen Elizabeth around this time brought Charles and Anne two South American love-birds which they named David and Annie. These they were allowed to have in the nursery on condition that they cleaned out the cage themselves. While the children were busy with sand, seed, and water, the two birds sat on the window ledge or fluttered around the room to the great alarm of Miss Anderson, who regarded them as 'horrid, vicious creatures', and was frightened that they would tangle themselves in her hair, like bats. As if aware of her fears, the birds would come swooping down on her with high-pitched adenoidal squawks. On one occasion she defended herself by smothering them in a blanket, only to whip it off again quickly when she thought of what a scandal *this* would build up into if the R.S.P.C.A. ever got to hear of it. The children, however, continued to assure her that the birds were charming pets, of the most docile disposition, and Anne eventually trained one of them to come and perch on a stick when she held it at arm's length.

At Balmoral there were the ponies. Charles had learned to ride before Miss Peebles appeared, taught by one of the grooms on an old Shetland pony called Fum that had been brought up from Sandringham. Afterwards Miss Sybil Smith, who had taught the Queen to ride, took over his tuition and Fum was replaced by a Welsh mountain pony named William, on which Charles would sometimes ride down to the village shop to buy ice-cream. He enjoyed being with horses, but was never swept away by the whole-hearted enthusiasm for them that his mother and sister have.

He had also been having dancing lessons. Miss Vacani, of the long-established dancing-school in London, came herself to the Palace to teach him and a small class made up by

King George and Prince Charles at Buckingham Palace

*Right:* January 27, 1951
*Below:* Prince Charles with the Queen, 1952
*Lower right:* Loch Muich, August 30, 1952
*Opposite:* August 31, 1952

The Queen with
Sir Winston Churchill,
Prince Charles and
Princess Anne
at Balmoral,
October 3, 1952

Winter at Sandringham,
1952

*Opposite:* Royal salute

In *Britannia*

*Opposite:* With Queen Elizabeth and Princess Anne, 1955

Hockey in
*Britannia*, 1956

inviting the children of some of the younger married couples among the Household officials and the Queen's friends. Miss Peebles found that he was a good natural dancer and already showed a strong sense of rhythm, one of the early indications of his gift for music.

By the time that Miss Peebles was installed in the nursery schoolroom and the lessons and timetable had been agreed on, the Queen and the Duke of Edinburgh were about to leave on a tour that would part them from the children for several months. It was, in fact, the ill-fated Commonwealth Tour which had been originally postponed in 1948, when the King's health had suddenly worsened, and had been interrupted in 1952 by his death when Princess Elizabeth had got no farther than Kenya. Now, leaving in November 1953, on a journey that would take them to ten Commonwealth countries and make the Queen the first reigning sovereign of any nationality to travel round the world, they were not expected home until May of the following year.

In most branches of the Royal Family, and in previous generations at the Palace itself, it was the custom to bring in children from outside to form a class and share the lessons with the young prince or princess. This is indeed the course that the Queen has adopted with her younger children. But she already saw that Charles was likely to get more embarrassment than encouragement from working as one of a group (looking back today he is certain that her assessment was right), and she consequently decided that, at least while he was with Miss Peebles, he should have his lessons alone (with the obvious exception of the dancing lessons, where, in any case, Charles forgot his selfconsciousness in the lilt of the music).

A good deal of what was important in his life was lived internally, within the bounds of his own imagination. Miss Peebles discovered that she had to deal with a vague child, or, perhaps more accurately, a child who still had only a vague relationship to the external world. He was reluctant to concentrate, not thirsty for knowledge, but on the other hand very conscientious. When he knew it was his duty to learn something, he set out determinedly to learn it. He was a plodder: when he knew where he had to go he would get there, somehow.

He could already tell the time, and his mother had taught him to read simple words. He could pencil out CHARLES in capital letters. He could draw rather better than the average boy of his age and was more ambitious than most in choosing horses and dogs as his favourite models. With his good ear for tunes went a promising treble voice.

Since his parents were away, it was Queen Elizabeth who kept a watchful eye on the early days of schooling. After a month at Buckingham Palace both children went to Sandringham for Christmas, where the presents from the Queen and the Duke had been wrapped and left in readiness, and on Christmas morning they were able to talk on the telephone with their parents, who had by then arrived in New Zealand—on the other side of the world. A globe was one of the earliest additions to the schoolroom equipment and Charles followed the grand tour on this with Miss Peebles's help. Geography is a subject that he has grown up with, rather than learned.

The royal yacht *Britannia* was to meet the Queen in the Mediterranean, and the children had been promised that they should go in her. On April 15 they drove down to Portsmouth with Queen Elizabeth to see them off and Miss Peebles, Mrs. Lightbody and Miss Anderson to go with them. Queen Elizabeth inspected the ship, the children's quarters and their supply of toys, and was piped ashore; and then they were off for Malta, escorted by a frigate of the Royal Navy. It took a day for them to get used to the motion of the ship (Charles's enthusiasm for his father's favourite sport of yachting would be greater if it were not for the fact that he gets seasick when the weather turns rough), but after that they managed to explore most of it, running barefoot most of the time with a couple of seamen as escorts and no interference from nurses or governesses except at mealtimes. There was a sand-box to dig in on the upper deck; a boat-shaped pedal car for Charles to speed around in; a new camera for him to take pictures. The frigate did impressively dashing manœuvres with foam curling up from her bows, and one day a life belt was dropped into the sea and boat's crews from *Britannia* and the frigate had a race to rescue the imaginary man overboard.

On April 22 they arrived at Malta, where their great-uncle, Admiral Lord Mountbatten, was commander-in-chief. He came on board with Lady Mountbatten to greet them, and during the next two or three days showed them round the island, recently battered by German bombers but with much older scars from the days when the Knights Hospitallers defended it against pirates and invaders from the East. This was the sort of rich, romantic stuff that was later to be Charles's delight and principal interest, but at the time his attention was easily diverted by the arrival in harbour of the aircraft carrier *Eagle* and an invitation to look round it.

*Britannia* took them on to Tobruk, where on May 2 the Queen was at last piped on board and could take them to her private quarters and give them a proper greeting after six months of separation. (Charles, watching what the officers were up to, had had to be dissuaded from joining the line to salute and shake hands with her when she came on board.) At Tobruk, King Idris of Libya made Charles a present of an Arab saddle and harness, upholstered in velvet and ornamented with gold and silver; at Gibraltar there was a model of the Rock, with clockwork trains running through the tunnel underneath it: a toy that was set up in the basement of Buckingham Palace and played with by many members of the Royal Family besides the children. At Gibraltar, too, there were the apes. Charles watched with amusement as they leaped on Anne's shoulder, and with undisguised dismay as they took the same liberty with Mrs. Lightbody.

Gibraltar was the last port of call on the historic voyage. A few days later there was a final hour of excitement, walking behind their parents to the reception by the dignitaries assembled on Westminster Pier, and driving through cheering crowds from there to the Palace; then the junketing was over and lessons began in earnest. Not that the timetable was particularly burdensome. There was still the half-hour with Mummy from nine to nine-thirty. Then lessons until eleven and, when he was a little older, noon. Walks were usually designed to combine information with exercise: down the Mall to the shipping offices in Cockspur Street, for instance, and a talk from Miss Peebles on the great trade routes; or to the farthest corner of the City, to be shown round the Tower by the Beefeaters; sometimes back through the familiar garden door into Clarence House, to go with Granny to watch Trooping the Colour and their mother taking the salute. That year Charles watched, from Catherine of Aragon's loft in St. George's Chapel, Windsor, the annual service of the Knights of the Garter. One day he would be the first of them in rank; as he looked down he saw Sir Winston Churchill walking in the procession for the first time, as the most junior.

When the family was at Windsor, Miss Peebles stayed at Royal Lodge and came up to the Castle every day to give Charles his lessons. Reading, as well as geography, came easily, though he still preferred somebody else to read to him at bedtime. With writing he had little difficulty. But arithmetic he found a monumental bore and inscrutable mystery. The Queen was not surprised; she shared the same blind spot. It has never worried her; she much prefers that her son should be interested in people rather than ciphers. And this interest in people was now being clearly expressed in the eagerness with which he approached his history lessons. Miss Peebles drew up a series of studies of 'children in history' so that he could see the story of England through the eyes of boys of his own age. The children were real; some of them had been sons of kings and queens; it was another step towards appreciating his own unique position.

Though Charles took his lessons alone, the Queen encouraged both of the children to see as much of their friends as possible outside school hours. Young visitors came to the Palace and the Castle for games in the afternoons; at holidays they were invited to Sandringham and Balmoral. Always, if the Queen or the Duke were in the building at all, they kept to the old rule of coming up after tea to play with the children, read them stories, see them to bed and say goodnight.

In the second year Miss Peebles added French to the curriculum, and the educational visits became more frequent and more essentially a part of the scheme of education. On April 11, 1955, the Queen's Press Secretary, Commander (now Sir) Richard Colville, sent a letter to newspaper editors, asking for their co-operation:

'I am commanded by the Queen to say that Her Majesty and the Duke of Edinburgh have decided that their son has reached the stage when he should take part in more grown-up educational pursuits with other children.

'In consequence, a certain amount of the Duke of Cornwall's instruction will take place outside his home; for example, he will visit museums and other places of interest. The Queen trusts, therefore, that His Royal Highness will be able to enjoy this in the same way as other children without the embarrassment of constant publicity. In this respect, Her Majesty feels that it is equally important that those in charge of, or sharing in, the instruction should be spared undue publicity, which can so seriously interrupt their normal lives.

'I would be grateful if you will communicate the above to your members and seek their co-operation in this matter, informing them at the same time that they are at liberty to publish this letter if they so wish.'

The request sprang from a growing sense of oppression in the Royal Family, an anxiety to find a way of letting Charles see a little of the world outside palaces without having him overwhelmed by the demands of reporters and photographers and the natural but unrestrained curiosity of ordinary folk. It partly succeeded in this object; but it also had the contrary effect of encouraging editors to supply public demand with stories that were entirely fictitious. They were mostly trivial and went uncontradicted; it is only in rare cases that the Royal Family is moved to issue denials. Meanwhile Charles added the Science and Natural History Museums to his list of cultural jaunts; Madame Tussaud's where there were wax figures of his mother and father; the planetarium next door where he was fascinated by the movement of the constellations. He is, as the Queen says, 'a country person' like herself and all the others of the family, and the stars were as familiar to him as the woods and fields and mountains of Norfolk and Aberdeenshire.

He was riding a good deal now, sometimes on William, the Welsh pony, sometimes on a Dartmoor pony which had been given to the Queen for him at the Royal Show of 1954. He enjoyed following the shooting parties at Sandringham, hobnobbing with the beaters quite as happily as with the guns, and insisting on his privilege of counting the bag. He and his sister took their first flight, from Balmoral to London, in June 1955, with Wing Commander John Crindon as pilot and Sir Edward Fielden, Captain of the Queen's Flight, sitting with them to explain the way things worked. At Balmoral the open-air life was at its most spacious. The children roamed at their will, not visibly supervised, though most of the time unknown to themselves a careful watch was being kept on them.

Their games were played with the royal cousins who came to stay and with the children of ghillies on the Balmoral estate. 'Witches' and 'Ring-a-ring-o'-roses' and a game called 'Stone' that was rather similar to 'He'.

In the summer of 1956 Prince Charles was inducted into the mysteries of cricket, and when he came back from Balmoral in the early autumn he had his first taste of Association Football. But he did not, then or at any time, take to team games with enthusiasm. He got far more enjoyment in the water than at the wicket or the goal. The Duke of Edinburgh had taken him in hand in the Buckingham Palace swimming pool almost as soon as he could walk; he was a competent swimmer well before he was six years old and now at seven he swam like a fish—or like his mother, who learned to swim when she was ten but quickly qualified for life-saving badges.

Within the family circle he and Princess Anne were showing an increasing interest in playing charades, and any other game that offered an excuse for dressing up. Discarded ceremonial clothes accumulate in royal households, and great chests of unwanted robes and uniforms were turned over to the children, who could disguise themselves rather more easily as the Cham of Tartary or the Queen of Sheba than as the desiccated civil servant whom Prince Charles was cast to play in a film that was rehearsed, but never in fact photographed. It was soon clear that Prince Charles had a natural gift for acting. Older members of the Household remembered that the Queen, at a rather later age than this, had had her successes on the stage in the famous Windsor pantomimes during the war. These had been originally organized with the concealed motive of helping her to overcome the shyness which had troubled her childhood and caused a little uneasiness to her parents. Prince Charles took to mime earlier and without any prompting; and, so long as the audience was composed only of family and close friends, without self-consciousness.

Meanwhile, the Queen had been considering the best method to give Charles the lessons in classes away from home that had been mentioned in Colville's letter to the press. One afternoon in the late autumn of 1956 Colonel Townend, founder and headmaster of a school in Hans Place, Knightsbridge, was invited to tea at Buckingham Palace and after a talk with the Queen asked to accept Charles as a pupil. The Colonel was immensely flattered by the compliment and profoundly worried by the implications. There was the responsibility of looking after the physical welfare of the Prince and the—rather remote—nightmare that somebody might trip him up and break his leg or bounce him on his head in the gymnasium. There was the more certain danger that the Prince's presence at the school would attract so much publicity and press activity that the education of all the other boys would suffer. However, this was not a boy to whose parents the Colonel could bring himself to say 'no'. With mixed feelings he accepted the task.

The Queen was as anxious as Colonel Townend that Charles's entry to the school—it is called Hill House—should be made with as little publicity as possible. The press soon got hold of a rumour that he was a pupil at the school, and the Queen decided that he should not attend at the beginning of the Michaelmas term. The school tailor came to the Palace to measure him for his school uniform; the date was kept secret but reporters and photographers still hung about the pavement outside Hill House. On November 7, 1956, his uniform hidden under an overcoat, Charles stepped into one of the less recognizable Palace cars with Miss Peebles and was driven to Hans Place. With other small boys being decanted at the entrance, and hurrying in, their faces half hidden by their school caps, there seemed no reason why Charles should not pass unnoticed. Instead, he had no sooner stepped out of the car than the photographers pounced. He was the only boy that day wearing an overcoat with a velvet collar.[1]

After that first day the intensity of the press siege of Hill House rapidly declined. There were only a few weeks left of the winter term; and during those weeks Prince Charles was not enrolled in any class. He continued his lessons with Miss Peebles in the morning, and went to Hill House only in the afternoons, to join in the school games, so that he could become accustomed to being one of a crowd of his contemporaries, and get the 'feel' of the place. Every afternoon a procession of small boys in cinnamon-coloured shorts and sweaters emerged from Hill House and marched two abreast, southward. They crossed the King's Road at a foot crossing, each boy gravely taking off his cap to any motorist who stopped to let them go by. Somewhere in the line was the Heir Apparent to the Throne, but nobody who did not personally know him was at all likely to pick him out. Neither the master in charge nor the boys in front or beside or behind him paid him any attention that might make him conspicuous. He had faded into his background as the Queen and Colonel Townend hoped.

The procession filed into the grounds of the Duke of York's Headquarters, the Chelsea military depot named after the son of George III who 'marched his men to the top of the hill And marched them down again'. Hill House had

1. It was not only newspapermen to whom the coat was familiar. In April 1954 *The Tailor and Cutter*, that austerely professional journal, which judges mankind as so many animated dummies for the display of the masterpieces of the craft, had placed Charles as first among the eleven best-dressed men of the year:

'His Baby-Bow and Fawn Stalker, followed by his junior fashion for a double-breasted woolly, is accentuated this year by his adoption of a very popular style among older folk. His velvet-collared topcoat also follows a popular current trend.'

the use of a part of the grounds to practise athletics and play games. At this time of the year the principal game was Soccer. Charles, with his lack of enthusiasm for almost all team games—the only notable exception was tug-of-war as a child and polo now that he has grown up—played dutifully but without much spirit. At his next school, Cheam, he began to find a little more pleasure in it and at Gordonstoun he was disappointed to find that they played Rugby football instead. But for the moment these afternoon activities rather bored him unless he was taking part in such things as running or jumping in which he could compete as an individual against individuals and not just as one of a team.

The end of this transitional term at Hill House also marks the end of Miss Peebles's official reign as Charles's governess, though she still remains one of his most trusted friends (he sent her long and lively letters from Australia, describing his experiences there). He was in his ninth year and it was time for him to cut free from petticoat influence. His father was away that winter, from October 1956 to February 1957, opening the Olympic Games at Melbourne and visiting the Antarctic; so Michael Farebrother, the young headmaster of St. Peter's School, Seaford, was brought to Sandringham to be Charles's 'holiday tutor' during the Christmas vacation. The purpose was mainly to give the boy some masculine companionship. The two of them roamed together on foot, on bicycles and on ponies over the bare fields and along the winterbound Norfolk roads. When the holiday was over, Charles was a little more prepared to face his first full day's work at school, away from home and among a class of comparative strangers.

\*     \*     \*

The Queen's decision to send Charles to Hill House as an ordinary member of the school was another break with tradition. In feudal times the sons of kings were often placed in the households of great noblemen, for education in chivalry. But the last instances of this were when the future Richard III was attached to the family of Richard Nevill, Earl of Warwick, 'The Kingmaker', and in Scotland when James VI, already King, was brought up by the Earl of Mar. From then onwards it had been the invariable custom for young princes to be educated at home, until Queen Victoria broke new ground.

She allowed her heir, Albert Edward, Prince of Wales, to go up to Christ Church, Oxford, and afterwards to Trinity College, Cambridge. But he was not permitted to live among ordinary undergraduates as one of themselves. A good deal of George V's education was gained at sea—where as a cadet he had his private tutors with him. His two sons, Edward VIII and George VI, passed through the Royal Naval College, Dartmouth, where the curriculum is roughly parallel to that of a public school; and afterwards went up to university and lived in college with their contemporaries, King Edward at Oxford, King George at Cambridge.[1] But no prince had ever yet attended a day school, and none began school life at anything like such an early age as eight.

The Queen had carefully considered and perfectly understood the implications of her breach of the old convention. Twelve years before she had set aside a similar convention affecting herself. According to the laws in force during the second world war a girl on reaching the age of eighteen was called up to one of the auxiliary services or equivalent work in aid of the war effort. The same birthday in the case of Princess Elizabeth made her eligible to act as a Counsellor of State during the King's absences from the country, and marked the stage at which many less solemn functions began to devolve upon her. The King, holding that these duties were quite enough to occupy her, gave directions that his

1. For the education of Edward VII and Edward VIII see the Appendix.

daughter should not be called up to any of the auxiliary forces. But Princess Elizabeth herself protested. The young women of her age were flocking to put on uniform, and she insisted that she could never fulfil her appointed role as the representative and leader of her generation unless she shared in the normal war experience of her contemporaries. She challenged her father directly, and he gave way. Princess Elizabeth received her commission as Second Subaltern in the Auxiliary Territorial Service, put on oily overalls, and was soon learning to cope with the maintenance of military lorries.

This was her first rebellion against the inherited limitations of royalty, and she must have remembered the occasion now, when she firmly and clearly decided that unless her son was brought up like other boys, who would one day be his subjects, he would never be able to make the contact with the ordinary man on which the service of kingship to the modern world depends.

Hill House was not, and is not, the sort of school that every ordinary boy attends. Although the Queen had taken the revolutionary step of sending her son to school ten years younger than any of his predecessors for the past five hundred years, there were still some people who criticized her for not having sent him to the nearest primary school like the son of the postman or the plumber. They argued that it was wrong to set him at an early age among the children of privileged families; and there is certainly no denying that the education Charles would get at Hill House was beyond the reach of most of the Queen's subjects.

The answer to the criticism that the Queen, by choosing this sort of school and this sort of education, was isolating her son from the majority of the people he would one day represent, is that, although the monarch has to represent all his people, that does not mean that he has to be exactly like them—an obvious impossibility in one man. He must keep an open mind and heart, so as to be ready to sympathize with all sorts of people; and in time, more than any other person in the land, he must get to know all kinds—but scarcely at eight years old! The ideal is that he shall grow up as an ordinary Englishman of his time—but an ordinary man in an extraordinary position. His people will wish to see in him a reflection of themselves—but of their best selves magnified and idealized. It is his business to show them, by a life lived largely in public, what they are, what the ordinary man is capable of becoming. That means that the two elements of the idea, the ordinary human being and the extraordinary position, are inseparable and equally important; and the education of a future king must take account of both.

Clearly, it must be the best general education available, given to the Prince not as a privilege for himself, but for the sake of his people, who do not wish to be represented by an illiterate sovereign. There are people who maintain that the best education in modern England is that which is provided by the State. It is not, however, the prevailing view, otherwise we should not hear so many complaints of the unfair advantages enjoyed in after life by the children of parents who can afford to pay for their education. The Queen, in sending her son to Hill House, was setting his foot on the first rung of a ladder which would lead up through a private preparatory school to a public school or similar institution and eventually to a university or service training college. This was the way, she judged, that would provide him with the opportunity to develop the capacities he would need for his career of public service; and all but a few eccentrics agreed that she was right.

For Prince Charles, more than for any other eight-year-old boy in the land, the nature of his future career was predetermined. That was the converse of his 'privileged' position: alone of his generation, he had no liberty to choose his course in life. It followed that he could and should be educated from the very beginning so as to fit him for his unique position. Sooner or later it might be desirable to deflect his studies in directions specially appropriate to that position. The Queen herself, for example, when being educated at home, was given special lessons by Sir Henry Marten, Provost of Eton, in the history and constitution of the Kingdom and Commonwealth over which she would one day reign—lessons which it was not thought necessary that even her sister Princess Margaret should share. Such special treatment for one individual pupil is something for which the curriculum of the L.C.C. Education Department did not provide. It can only be arranged in what is called the 'private sector'. It was clearly better that Prince Charles should enter this private sector 'on the ground floor'.

The other objection to a state education was in a sense the converse of this. Against all the influences working to set him apart from his contemporaries, the Queen was resolved to do all in her power to bring her son up as an ordinary boy; and paradoxical as it might seem, the state school was the place where he would have least chance of getting an ordinary education. Compared with Hill House, in its secluded corner of Hans Place, the council school had far less effective defences to keep at bay those who would inevitably come crowding for a glimpse of the Prince. Its teachers would be more likely to be overawed by their responsibility; the other children, drawn from much humbler strata of society, would be more inclined to treat him as a fabulous animal coming from an unknown world. Not only would the emphasis on his peculiar position, which the Queen wished to play down, be reasserted: his presence would be a disturbing influence in the school itself and react adversely on the education of his fellow-pupils.

The story is told of the late Sir Herbert Warren, President

of Magdalen, equally famous for his scholarship and his adulation of the great, that he was one day discussing with the Japanese Ambassador the arrangements for the admission of the young son of the Mikado. 'What is he called in his own country?' said Warren. 'At home, of course, it is etiquette to address him as the son of God.' 'That will cause no difficulty,' the President is alleged to have replied, 'we are accustomed to the sons of important personages at Magdalen.'

No such ceremony was expected for the new boy at Hill House. Everybody at Buckingham Palace, from the nursery page upwards, called him simply 'Charles', and the Queen wished him to go on being addressed in the same way at school. Nevertheless, one of the advantages of Hill House[1] was that it was accustomed to receiving the sons of people of some worldly importance, and therefore Prince Charles would not stand out from his surroundings as he might have done in a less fashionable establishment. It was also much favoured by members of the Diplomatic Corps posted to London with young children to educate. These foreign children, in Prince Charles's time, accounted for about a third of the whole school, and were another of the elements that weighed with the Queen in choosing Hill House: Charles would be thrown into the company of boys from half the countries of Europe and from as far afield as South America.

Colonel Townend had been at pains to prepare the way tactfully for the arrival of his unusual pupil. The boys knew Prince Charles was coming, although the date was kept dark from them as from everybody else. The headmaster told

1. Hill House has developed a good deal since Prince Charles's day. It now has a sort of colony at Glion, in Switzerland, and whole classes are switched about between there and Hans Place for a few weeks at a time. It also keeps its pupils to a later age than it did in 1957. At that time it was regarded as a 'pre-preparatory' school for boys not yet old enough to be sent to the country as boarders.

them that they must not regard their new schoolfellow as an exceptionally privileged person. On the contrary, he said, it was they who were privileged, because they were free to make their own lives, while he was already living in the strait-jacket of ceremonial and royal security precautions. As a result of these admonitions, the other boys, when Prince Charles did arrive, treated him with remarkable kindness—which is not by any means the universal reaction of eight-and nine-year-olds to a newcomer who does not conform precisely to their own pattern.

And it has to be admitted that, through no fault of his own, Prince Charles at first did not quite conform to type. Despite all the efforts his parents, nurses, governesses and holiday tutor had devoted to making him or keeping him a natural boy, Buckingham Palace and Windsor Castle are not the houses in which the general run of natural boys spend their infancy and the differences engendered by the unusual environment were bound to show. For example, he had never been inside a shop. He knew nothing about money and had never handled it. One of the first tasks of the school was to teach him the values of these various bronze and cupro-nickel discs with his mother's head on them. And it was not until six months after he went to Hill House that he made his first journey on a bus.

The school of about a hundred and fifty boys was run on pleasantly domesticated lines. Colonel Townend believes in discipline for the young; but he aims at the discipline of a family rather than an institution, and regards himself as a universal father. There is also a mother: Mrs. Townend plays an indispensable part in the running of the place. It was she who designed the school uniform of cinnamon-coloured sweater, shorts, blazer and cap. One of her new duties was to take turns with her husband at waiting in the entrance hall to receive Prince Charles on his arrival every morning, with no other escort than the chauffeur. They were not there with any idea of ceremony, but to guard against news-hungry intruders.[1]

Colonel Townend lives informally among his large family. They speak not only to him, but of him, simply as 'Sir'. You hear such remarks as 'Have you seen Sir about anywhere?' 'No, I've just been to the gymnasium, but Sir wasn't there.' He does not usually take his meals with the boys, but in a dining room of his own, where he can enter-tain a guest. But the room is little more than a passage wide enough to take a small table. The house is not big enough for everybody to eat at once: the boys go to their luncheon in relays, class by class, and they go streaming back and forth through the headmaster's 'dining room', grinning cheerfully at him as he sits at table and stopping for a mo-ment to answer any remark that 'Sir' may address to a boy as the queue passes.

'Sir' has the kind of natural authority that reduces even small boys to quiet and orderly behaviour in his presence. His first principle of discipline is 'leadership from the front by example'. There is no corporal punishment, but occasi-onally 'lines' are awarded. The worst crime known to the Hill House code is disgracing the uniform in public; this entails the worst of its punishments, confiscation of the school tie. Prince Charles was no impeccable model of propriety. Whenever there was a rumpus in the classroom he was fairly certain to be in it. But he never lost his tie.

Colonel Townend was an Oxford Blue at Association football, president of the university athletic club, a gold medallist member of the British Empire team, and winner

1. Once inside the doors of Hill House, Prince Charles was protected within a barrier of extreme discretion, not because he was the Queen's son but because that is the tradition of this most discreet establishment. The rule is that nothing is disclosed about any boy to anyone but his parents; and it was only after special permission had been obtained from Bucking-ham Palace that Colonel Townend consented to draw on his memory to help the compilation of this book.

of another gold medal for ski-running in Switzerland. He himself taught Prince Charles Latin, which was a new subject to the boy, and coached him in all games. For other subjects Prince Charles sat under 'tutors', as Hill House calls its teaching staff, most of whom for boys as small as Prince Charles were ladies. A great deal of encouragement was given to drawing, and this was very much to the taste of the new boy, who had already covered reams of paper with pencil and brush in the nursery at Buckingham Palace.[1]

Another subject was elementary anatomy. This was taught to him by Mrs. Townend, who before her marriage had been theatre sister at Guy's Hospital to Sir John Weir, who had been present at Charles's birth. As she remembers the lessons now, they consisted mainly of lying on her back on the floor for her young pupil to practise artificial respiration. As a memorial of the time he spent under her care, she keeps a small square stool, five inches high from the ground, on which he used to sit every Friday evening when he came to tea with her before being fetched by the royal chauffeur to take him off to Windsor for the weekend.

Prince Charles made an unfortunate start with his Hill House career. At the end of his first week he went down with tonsillitis, which kept him away from school for three weeks. After that he settled down to his lessons very smoothly. In his second term he learned to play cricket. There is no boxing at Hill House, but wrestling is encouraged, and this for a time became Prince Charles's favourite sport.

On the playing field, this first term was largely devoted to preparation for 'Field Day', the annual sports meeting. The Queen came to watch, and enjoyed herself no less for seeing

1. His very first lesson at Hill House seems to have been devoted to the water-colour depiction of a green ship sailing under a bridge. This masterpiece does not survive.

her son come toiling in with the 'also rans'. It was one of the
rare occasions in London when she could unbend completely. The order had gone out that there was to be no
formality to distinguish her from any other parent among
the spectators. But one exception was made: Prince Charles
was allowed to line up the members of his own class and
present them one by one to his mother. It appears to have
been his very first introduction to court protocol.

Hill House sets examinations at the end of each term, but
parents are not told the results. These are posted up on the
school notice board, and parents are at liberty to come in
and look at them if they feel so disposed. Neither the Queen
nor the Duke of Edinburgh chose to make the journey, and
the Prince of Wales no longer remembers how he got on at
his first test. But his first school report, signed by 'Sir', does
still survive:

Lent 1957, Upper VI.
Reading—Very good indeed. Good expression.
Writing—Good. Firm, Clear, well formed.
Arithmetic—Below form average. Careful but slow—not
    very keen.
Scripture—Shows keen interest.
Geography—Good.
History—Loves this subject.
French—Shows promise.
Latin—Made a fair start.
Art—Good, and simply loves drawing and painting.
Singing—A sweet voice, especially in lower register.
Football—enjoying the game.
Gymnastics—Good.
                          Henry Townend, Headmaster

Colonel Townend found Prince Charles 'tremendously
observant', that he had perfect manners, never asserted his

rank, and was never cheeky to the staff. Prince Charles's memory is that at this age he still scarcely realized that he had any rank to assert. As to not being cheeky to the staff, he had before this been pretty heavily dropped on by his father for occasional thoughtless rudeness to Palace servants, and the lesson had no doubt sunk in.

The second term at Hill House, like the first, was interrupted near the beginning by an attack of tonsillitis. This time the tonsils came out. The operation was performed in Buckingham Palace, and afterwards Charles was sent for convalescence to Holkham Hall, the historic home of the Cokes, earls of Leicester. Lady Leicester was an old friend, having been—as she still is—Lady in Waiting to the Queen since just before the Coronation; and Holkham is close enough to Sandringham (which at that time of the year was closed) to make him feel at home. The sea air of Norfolk quickly restored him to health, and he was back at Hill House in the latter part of May. The tonsils, which Prince Charles had begged from the surgeon, were preserved in spirits and proudly shown to visitors to the Palace nursery; but he was not allowed to take them to school.

During the rest of that summer term Prince Charles learned to handle a cricket bat, but scored few runs and took few wickets. He continued to make unspectacular progress with his lessons and finished with a report very like that of his first term. Arithmetic remained an intolerable stumbling block, drawing and painting his chief talent and interest. He was less shy now than he had been as a new boy and had begun to acquire some special friends in the school, particularly the young son of Canon Carpenter of Westminster. This was his last term at Hill House. He left behind the impression that he was a little above average intelligence, with some creative capacity perhaps inherited from his father, and with his mother's receptive mind though not her quickness of apprehension. The Queen herself judges her son to have been a slow developer; but he was determined and, unlike some others with more spectacular gifts, what he absorbed he retained.

By August he had exchanged the Hill House cap for a blue yachting one and was on board the *Bluebottle* at Cowes. As they came back from their first race, the Duke allowed him to take over the helm. It had been an exciting day's sport and a pleasant one, but he still had not overcome his tendency to seasickness in rough weather. His pleasure in sailing, first in *Bluebottle* and later in *Bloodhound*, sprang mainly from the fact that this was his father's favourite relaxation. Being close to his father was of great importance to him in childhood, and nowhere was he closer than when they were at sea. With the photographers usually far away, they could be as informal as they pleased. Skipper, crew and passengers all sat down to meals together and nobody made any bones about accepting a small boy, not yet nine, as a fully fledged seaman. By the time the holiday ended and they moved up to Balmoral, he was beginning to feel that he counted in the grown-up world.

A new kilt awaited him there, of 'large hunting pink squares with smaller lime-green check and intervening lines of lime-green and white'—the Rothesay tartan, though not named after him as Duke: it was first spun and woven at Rothesay by the late Lord Bute. Very elegant, if you enjoyed dressing up—and he did. And another indication that childhood was ending. This autumn he would be away at school not just for a day at a time but for a whole term.

## { 3 }

# AWAY TO SCHOOL

IN the year 1665 the Great Plague fell upon London and
struck terror into the heart of most of the citizens, including the Reverend George Aldritch, who kept a small private
school for the sons of the nobility and gentry. He packed up
his school, lock, stock and barrel, and took himself off with
his pupils to the little market town of Cheam in Surrey.
There he amalgamated with a local school already established
in a house called Whitehall, which still stands in the High
Street. This school, whose old boys were matriculating at
Oxford and Cambridge during the Civil War, must have
been in existence well back in the reign of Charles I.

The plague came to an end, but Mr. Aldritch never
returned to London. The combined school made several
moves within the boundaries of Cheam; but from 1719 to
1934 it remained in one place, near the modern railway
station. Then, to avoid being swallowed up in the tide of
urbanization that came swelling out from London, it packed
up again and moved to its present home at Headley, on the
Berkshire Downs. But it still clings to its ancient name of
Cheam.

In 1752 the school, which then had fifteen pupils, was

bought by a clergyman named William Gilpin who introduced several revolutionary reforms, the most notable of
them being an entirely new approach to punishment.
Eighteenth-century schoolmasters were convinced that
learning had to be beaten into boys. Gilpin on the contrary
seldom flogged his pupils; he drew up a list of crimes and
their appropriate punishments so that he should never be
carried to excesses by rage—and on the few occasions when
he did forget his rules the pupils were not afraid to stand up
and remind him. The school was reorganized in 1855 by a
headmaster named Tabor to prepare boys for entry to the
public schools, and now has claims to be considered the
oldest preparatory school in England. Its records show the
names of many distinguished alumni, including Lord
Randolph Churchill, father of Sir Winston, Lord Willing-
don and Lord Hardinge of Penshurst, Viceroys of India, Sir
Ian Hamilton, military commander-in-chief of the ill-fated
Gallipoli expedition, Lord Dunsany, the Irish writer, and
Lord Ruffside, best remembered as Mr. Speaker Clifton-
Brown. But in 1957 the most exalted old boy appeared in
the books as Prince Philip of Greece and Denmark, who was
now His Royal Highness the Duke of Edinburgh.

As Prince Charles's stay at Hill House neared its end the
Queen and the Duke of Edinburgh had many serious dis-
cussions about where their son should go next. He was
clearly committed to school education: it would be impossible now to go back to home tutors. Nor indeed had that
ever been the Queen's idea: she wants her son to grow up as
an ordinary Englishman of his time, and takes the common-
sense view that, since we have an excellent school system in
this country, it would be foolish not to make use of it. She
was looking for a middle-of-the-road school. Not one preparing for a particular public school, since there had not yet
been any decision about Prince Charles's further destination;
not a 'cramming' school, devoted to breeding successful

examinees; certainly not one committed to any of the
elaborate educational theories which their friends call advanced and their critics call cranky. During the months
when she was making up her mind, she contrived on more
or less transparent excuses to visit several possible places, to
look at the buildings, talk to the masters, and ask the sort of
questions expected of visiting royalty about the subjects
taught and the way the place was run. The press eagerly
noted each move, and one school after another was confidently predicted as the likely choice for Prince Charles.
With less publicity, a number of schoolmasters received
invitations to those informal luncheon parties at Buckingham Palace which the Queen first instituted in May 1956
and which remain her favourite device for broadening her
acquaintance among the kind of people who have no
official status or functions to bring them into her presence.

None of them, evidently, presented so good a case for
their schools as did the distinguished old boy of Cheam who
is always at her side. Without even calling the joint headmasters, Mark Wheeler and Peter Beck, to luncheon, the
Queen decided that Charles should go to his father's old
school, and then led a family expedition to inspect the place,
accompanied by the Duke and both Charles and Anne.
They looked over the classrooms and dormitories and the
sixty-five acres of grounds. These, though they would put
plenty of distance between the new boy and roving press-
men, were also sufficiently studded with trees and shrubberies to allow anybody who did manage to get in to make
good use of a camera. It was decided that, at any rate for the
early days, a detective should be brought down to live in a
cottage in the grounds.

During the holiday at Balmoral, Charles's French was
strengthened with the help of Mlle Bibiane de Roujoux, who
had been recommended to the Queen by her own former
teacher, the Vicomtesse de Bellaigue, now Mrs. Ladd. He

had made some progress with the language at Hill House and the Queen felt that if he could be really outstanding in it by the time he went to Cheam it would help to give him confidence. So Mlle de Roujoux became companion as well as tutor and, whenever possible, luncheon was made a meal at which only French was spoken.

But however well his French may have developed, the approach of September and departure for Cheam was obviously producing acute nervous stress. He had always been, and remains, a home-loving boy. The Queen remembers that when the time came to leave Balmoral he shuddered with apprehension. The long overnight train journey to London was followed by a sixty-mile car drive to Headley with both his mother and father coming to see him safely into the school. (The nervous tension was not his alone. The Queen was as disquieted as any other mother at sending her eight-year-old son away to school for the first time. One of her hardest tasks has been to resist the temptation to accept special privileges for Charles, which have been so willingly offered but would have obstructed her desire for him to grow up in as ordinary an atmosphere as possible. She was careful not to express any wishes except that he should be treated exactly like any other boy; she made a point of not visiting the school any more frequently than other parents. Yet those close to her noticed the eagerness with which she listened to any scrap of information that came from Cheam.)

Charles was consigned to the care of the headmasters and his parents drove away. Some time later the mathematics master, David Munir, who had been told to keep a special eye on the Prince, went out into the grounds, which were in the usual beginning-of-term commotion and uproar. Standing apart, very much alone and very miserable, was one small boy 'notably in need of a haircut'. Munir did not need telling that this was Prince Charles. (Here, as at Hill House, the practice was for the staff to address him as 'Prince

Charles', the boys simply as 'Charles'. He used only his Christian name in signing his schoolwork—and still does today in signing cheques or documents—never adding the 'P', for *princeps*, even when he became entitled to do so on being created Prince of Wales.) The other boys were not boycotting him. They knew who he was and were over-awed by his position. The future King of England was too exotic an animal in the juvenile zoo for the rest to dare to approach him.

The problem had been partly foreseen. During the holidays, Mark Wheeler and Peter Beck had written to all the parents, telling them that Prince Charles would be joining the school next term and that 'it is the wish of the Queen and Prince Philip that there shall be no alteration in the way the school is run and that Prince Charles shall be treated the same as other boys. . . . It will be a great help if you will explain this. . . . His parents' wishes are that he should be given exactly the same education and upbringing as the other boys at the school.' The parents no doubt did explain this to their sons. But in fact it was no use pretending that the Queen's only son *was* an ordinary boy. The others could not quite believe it—and neither, now, could he.

This was the period during which, Prince Charles now recalls, he suffered the greatest embarrassment at being who he was, although it has by no means all disappeared today. But looking back he feels that the boys at Hill House were too young to pay much attention to his special position, and by the time he went to Gordonstoun he had conquered a great deal of his own diffidence—it was at Cheam that the problem presented itself in its most acute form. Quite simply, he had developed so shy a nature—perhaps because of a rather sheltered upbringing—that he found it almost impossible to push his way into a group of potential friends. And they, conscious of who he was, did not dare offer their friendship for fear that he or the other boys would think they were 'sucking-up'. Even the masters, asked by Charles's parents not to show him any special interest or favours, tended to remain a little more aloof from him than from other boys.

A great deal of his uneasiness he managed to conceal. In fact, he disguised it so well that, although he himself still vividly remembers the trials of the period he spent at Cheam, he is not remembered at the school as being anything of a lone wolf—except for the first few moments of his first day. David Munir rescued him from solitude, introduced him to some of the others, and he went on in time to make one or two close friends: Charles Donald, for instance, who went on to Harrow, and Christopher Wilson, who went to Stowe. And Mary Beck, the headmaster's daughter and only girl in the school. She was just Charles's age and was put in the same class. They went up the school together and she remembers him for his easy friendliness; if he was inwardly feeling that he was not fully accepted, it never showed in his demeanour. Mary's father, indeed, sums the Prince up as a very good mixer who was popular with all the boys. The fact seems to be that he was, as his mother and all who saw him in the nursery agree, unusually sensitive as a child, and it may well have been largely in his imagination that the other boys shrank away from him. The impressive thing is that, with this conviction so strong in him, he nevertheless managed to conceal his feelings and put the others at their ease.

There were, of course, distractions in the new way of life —and difficulties of a more material and less worrying kind. School meals brought a quite unexpected reaction from him. Early in his first term he found he had a stomach upset and went to consult the 'governess', Miss Cowlishaw. The trouble, he confided in her, was that at home he wasn't accustomed to all this rich food. But his digestion soon adjusted itself and his normal hearty appetite returned. He was fond of eating, as was apparent from his plump contours, and he often let his mind dwell on the subject.

One day a visiting clergyman talked to the boys about the Church, comparing it to a ship, and preparing to make the point that Jesus was its master. 'And who,' he asked, 'is the most important member of the crew?'

There was no reply.

'Come, come,' he said, 'it begins with a C.'

Several hands were raised. The clergyman pointed to a small plump boy in the front row.

'Please, sir,' said Prince Charles, 'the cook.'[1]

Charles was now, for the first time in his life, sleeping in an austere room with no carpet on the boards. There was an unyielding mattress on the ancient bed, which he was expected to make each morning. At night he had to clean his own shoes and take his turn in tidying the classroom. But he was a conscientious child and tackled the tasks eagerly. Not long after the beginning of term, David Munir came upon him downstairs, still busy with his chores when he should have been in bed long ago. Munir warned him that he would be getting into trouble with Matron, but Charles replied, 'I can't help that, sir; I must do my duties.'

The Cheam day began at a quarter past seven, with a master summoning the dormitory to 'Rise and shine'. Washed and dressed in their grey suits with short trousers (for outdoor wear they had royal blue caps initialled C and blazers with the monogram CS) the boys presented themselves for inspection by the Matron. Charles, always a tidy child, had no difficulty here. Mary Beck remembers that his fingernails, seldom a showpiece with small boys, were so well kept that she envied them. After Matron's inspection came prayers, a formal handshake with one of the headmasters, and then breakfast, at which each boy took his turn

1. This story is derived from an eye-witness, whose memory, nevertheless, the Prince of Wales believes to be at fault.

at waiting on table. Morning school began at nine and, with a morning break for milk, lasted through five teaching periods until lunchtime.

There is nothing in the Cheam curriculum to mark it out from that of any other preparatory school. All of them are dominated by the requirements of the Common Entrance examination which a boy must pass if he is to get a place at most public schools. Charles's future was not yet determined—and, as it turned out, he went to a school that does not make use of the examination—but his lessons followed the standard pattern. The numbering of classes at Cheam is from the top downwards and Charles consequently began in VII and eventually arrived at I (b). In French, thanks to Mlle de Roujoux, he was well away. He did not add much to his smattering of Latin, and did no Greek at all. Peter Beck was pleased to discover that he really did speak and write the Queen's English and not the usual small boys' careless slang. But it was becoming increasingly evident that his strongest subject was History.

He had an obvious advantage. History to the average child is about the apparently unmotivated movements of the scarcely animated puppets called Kings and Queens. For Charles it was a collection of tales about grandfather, or great-great-great-grandmother—or people from even remoter ages whose blood, he knew, still ran in his veins. (Later it came to have another, less comfortable, significance. He began to realize that history, which in the textbooks is about his ancestors, will one day be about him There have been times when he has been oppressed by the thought that some casual action may get confused with national affairs, that when he writes an informal letter to his mother or a friend it may somehow get swept up into the archives and provide raw material for some future historian.)

There remained one subject that he positively dreaded.

Mathematics were the source of even more labour and sorrow than they had been at Hill House. It was for this reason that David Munir, the mathematics master, had been asked to keep a special eye on him; and Charles's faltering path through the thickets of quadratic equations and Pons Asinorum brought pain and grief to both of them. It was also the one subject where even the Prince's usual conscientiousness deserted him. When Munir was talking to the Queen after Charles had been away from school for an operation for appendicitis towards the end of his stay at Cheam, he said, 'At least the convalescence has given him time to brush up on some subject for the Common Entrance. He tells me he has done a little mathematics, though not much.'

The Queen bubbled with laughter and told Munir that Charles had not opened a mathematics book the whole of the time. She confessed that she herself had very little idea of mathematics, and it looked as though Charles had even less. She evidently did not consider that this blank spot in her knowledge presented any great threat to the success of her reign. There is, after all, no clause in the Act of Settlement that the Sovereign shall be able to do sums.

Lessons filled a greater part of the day at Cheam than they had at Hill House, but there was still a lot of time for outdoor activities. The school was run on lines that owed a great deal to Baden Powell's theories on training boys, although it did not in fact have any official scout patrols; and afternoons when there were no lessons were not devoted solely to games with bat and ball. The boys were encouraged to acquire practical skills: woodcraft and cooking in the open air, knowledge of wild life, animal and vegetable, a kind of juvenile survival course, during which Charles, in addition to more mundane tasks, went hunting bears with the red water pistol that he had bought 'for shooting frogs' and built wigwams in the shrubberies.

From wigwams and water pistols to scalping was only a short step. Though Charles was unfailingly respectful to members of the staff (at least when they were present) he saw no reason to show deference to his contemporaries. When a fracas arose he was sure to be in it, and equally certain to give as good as he got. His shyness did not spring from timidity: when tempers began to rise he made good use of the wrestling that he had practised in the gymnasium at Hill House. The Cheam gymnasium became one of his favourite haunts. On one occasion, when the Queen was paying a visit, Peter Beck found mother and son playing happily among the parallel bars, rings and vaulting horse. As well as for pleasure, Charles used the equipment in a serious attempt to get rid of his puppy fat. He was still eating as heartily as ever and had recently been seen to be quite piqued when a voice below him in a collapsed scrum called, 'Oh, get *off* me, Fatty!'

During the first term that he was at Cheam the problem of press intrusion became more acute than ever before. Out of a total of eighty-eight days, there were only twenty on which one or other of the national newspapers did not carry a story about the Prince, his school, his companions or his teachers. The detective in the grounds could keep the reporters and photographers out, but he had no power to restrain the imagination of some of the papers' contributors. It was generally, and unfairly, assumed that either the boys or their parents or the staff had been talking; the suspicion disturbed their relations with each other; and there was the horrid prospect that this state of affairs would continue for the next four years until Charles left.

As a result, Richard Colville, the Queen's Press Secretary, asked the editors of the London newspapers to meet him during the Christmas holidays at Buckingham Palace, where

Peter Beck gave them a picture of the demoralization and unhappiness that were beginning to hang over Cheam because of the sense of being continually watched and, in some cases, offered bribes. Colville made it plain that unless this pursuit of petty little paragraphs ceased, the Queen would be forced to take Prince Charles away from school and have him educated privately—for the sake of all the other people involved as well as himself. The editors took the point and from then onwards printed only the genuine and important news about the Prince, as was their right.

There was good reason to write about him in the summer of 1958, the last term of his first year at Cheam. The Commonwealth Games, at Cardiff, were to be opened and presided over by the Queen; but sinus trouble which had been bothering her for some time suddenly flared up and she had to have an immediate operation. The Duke of Edinburgh took her place and it was announced that she would address the competitors and spectators in a recorded message at the end of the games. Prince Charles and some of the other boys were invited to watch the ceremony on television in the headmaster's study.

The stadium was packed. The Queen's voice came over clearly:

'The British Empire and Commonwealth Games in the capital,' she concluded, 'together with all the activities of the Festival of Wales, have made this a memorable year for the Principality. I have therefore decided to mark it further by an act which will, I hope, give as much pleasure to all Welshmen as it does to me. I intend to create my son Charles, Prince of Wales today.'

There was a great storm of applause and then thirty thousand Welsh voices suddenly mingled in harmony in 'God Bless the Prince of Wales'. When at last the company fell silent the record of the Queen's voice was resumed with: 'When he is grown up I will present him to you at

Caernarvon.' In the headmaster's study the other boys turned towards Charles, clapping and cheering. Peter Beck, who had been let into the secret beforehand, was watching the Prince and saw the look of acute embarrassment that flashed across his face. The incident remains in the Prince's mind, not simply because it was the moment he received a title that he was in any case sure he would one day have, but because it was then that he fully realized the loneliness of his position and the 'awful fate' that lay in store for him. He was nine years and eight months old.

In due course letters patent passed the Great Seal creating His Royal Highness Charles, Duke of Cornwall, to be Prince of Wales and Earl of Chester. The Earldom of Chester is the oldest of all the dignities of the Heir Apparent. It was surrendered to the Crown when the palatinate originally created for Hugh of Avranches, nephew of William the Conqueror, was divided among coheiresses in 1242. It was bestowed in 1254 on the future Edward I, and since then has always been given with the Principality of Wales. But unlike the dukedom of Cornwall, which is entailed by charter on the Sovereign's eldest son from birth, or from his parent's accession, the earldom is treated as an ordinary peerage, which merges in the Crown when its holder becomes King and has to be re-created for the next incumbent.

In acquiring the rank of Prince of Wales the Prince auto-matically became a Knight of the Garter, the oldest secular Order of Chivalry in Europe, whose statutes lay down that the Sovereign and the Prince of Wales are constituent parts of the Order, which is made up of these two and twenty-four knights companions. The second stall in St. George's Chapel, Windsor, is the Prince's stall; but he cannot occupy it or wear the gorgeous insignia of the Garter until he has been dubbed knight by the Sovereign; and the Queen, anxious as ever to delay the involvement of her son in the pomp and burdens of public life, has been in no hurry to perform this ceremony.

That day, July 26, 1958, completed the roll of titles of the heir apparent to the English and Scottish throne. He was now for state documents His Royal Highness Prince Charles Philip Arthur George, Prince of Wales and Earl of Chester, Duke of Cornwall, Duke of Rothesay, Earl of Carrick, Lord of the Isles and Baron of Renfrew, Prince and Great Steward of Scotland, Knight Companion of the Most Noble Order of the Garter. After the usual holiday at Balmoral, showing off a little now to sister Anne, who had not yet attained the dignity of a schoolgirl, he was back at school for the Christmas term as merely Charles, still very much a junior, wrestling with simple equations and doing his daily chores. There was only one improvement of status— another generation of new boys had arrived, and from the lofty eminence of a second-year boy he could now patronize them.

His scholastic progress over the next four years was exactly like that of the other ninety boys in the school, and of the thousands of others in preparatory schools up and down the land who are reasonably sure to qualify without cramming for entry to a public school, but are not expected to achieve the distinction of a scholarship. There was never any doubt that the Prince had the capacity to reach the required standard. Peter Beck sums it up by saying that he was above average in intelligence, but only average in attainment. This looks at first sight like a schoolmasterly way of saying politely that he was clever but idle. But it is not. The judgment, which relates solely to classroom work, chimes with the impression formed by Colonel Miller, the Crown Equerry, to whom the Prince was sent in the holidays, towards the end of his time at Cheam, to be coached in the finer points of horsemanship. Colonel Miller's opinion was that the Prince of Wales might well fail at O-levels in French or Latin (in this he turned out to be wrong), but that in general knowledge he was decidedly ahead of most boys of his age. He had an interest in a great variety of subjects, and though a little shy was very well able to take care of himself in conversation with adults. Comparing the two opinions, the inference is that it was the out-of-class activities and non-academic interests at Cheam that predominated in developing Prince Charles's mind and character. If this meant that he was expanding his range of interests at the expense of depth in the subjects that go down in examination papers, it was no bad thing in a boy who would in later life have to strive to be all things to all men.

Despite his inner misgivings, he was trying to be a sociable child. In his second year he was accepted on equal terms by his companions, and in a modest way could sometimes lead them. Preparatory schools are at the mercy of the fashionable winds of change. They are swept by irresistible though short-lived 'crazes'—for Yo-yo or Pogo, model aircraft or roller skates. Birthday presents may start one of these epidemics. The Queen saw to it that her son's presents, or at any rate those which were sent to him at school, were no more pretentious than those of other boys; but they tended to set a fashion. Mary Beck remembers a rather elaborate pencil box he was given: immediately every other boy who wanted to be in the swim had to have one like it. She recalls also a peculiar toy of his called a doodle-master, which could draw complicated patterns on paper: before long there was one in every locker. While he could occasionally lead fashion, he could also resist. When 'bug-hunting' came into vogue, he chose not to join in. Nor did he ever become a stamp collector—perhaps because he knew that his mother had inherited from her grandfather the finest collection in the world, and it would be slightly absurd to compete.

He began to play the piano, the first of a series of musical

instruments at which he tried his hand. He had a clear treble
voice, and sang in the choir at school services at the village
church of St. Peter's, Headley. He had retained his delight
in colour and form, continuing to draw and paint at every
opportunity, and regularly showing his work at the school
art exhibition. This was not the only way in which he could
work with his hands: he joined the carpentry class and
produced an elegant table which is still among Princess
Anne's valuable possessions. At the Under-10 modelling
exhibition he was commended for a work grimly described
as 'Gallows and Stocks'.

There is no permanent stage at Cheam for theatrical performances, but one can be rigged up in the School Room
when required, and David Munir was in the habit of writing
plays for the boys to perform there. The privilege of taking
part is confined to the three senior forms, so the Prince's
career as an actor did not begin until he was half-way
through his time at school; but when it did he took to it like
a duck to water.

He was younger than his mother had been when she first
appeared in the series of Windsor pantomimes, from *The
Sleeping Beauty* in 1942 to *Old Mother Red Riding Boots* in
1944, which had been devised partly with the aim of helping
her to overcome her shyness. And certainly the Cheam plays
were not specially adapted with one boy in mind, but
Munir did try to fit the lines to the actor who was cast to
speak them. Unfortunately, chance sometimes played odd
tricks.

In *The Last Baron* the boy who should have played the
Duke of Gloucester, afterwards Richard III, left unexpectedly and had to be replaced by his understudy, Prince
Charles. The part turned out to be full of lines that suddenly
became unsuitable, such as Richard's prayer, 'and soon may
I ascend the Throne'. Charles, modelling his performance
on that of Sir Laurence Olivier in a more widely known

production, carried the part off with great aplomb, despite the occasional laugh at an incongruous line.

Under the first Elizabeth, a play with so many double meanings as this had suddenly developed could well have had the actor in the Tower and the author on his way to the block. But her successor on the Throne was unable to attend this performance at Cheam. The date was February 19, 1960, and while the Prince of Wales was still on the stage the headmaster entered to announce the birth of his brother, Prince Andrew.

This was a great event in the life of the Prince of Wales, still very much a home-loving boy with a highly developed sense of family. The Queen had told him in August that an addition to the circle was expected, and both he and Princess Anne had hoped for a brother rather than a sister. At first, feeling the weight of his own eleven years, he worried a little about the infant's future, with nobody of his own age to play with. 'Mummy will have to have another baby soon,' he remarked to a member of the Household. Meanwhile he was ready to lend a hand with all the new domestic duties. Though he had moved into a room of his own on the top floor of Buckingham Palace, he was constantly in and out of the nursery and took a special delight in bathing his baby brother himself. And back at school he missed no opportunity to pass round stories about Prince Andrew, whether derived from personal observation or from the long letters that both his parents, even when the business of state was most pressing, wrote to him several times a week.

The outdoor life of Cheam was specially important to the Prince of Wales, partly because he loved it, having been brought up as a countryman by a country-loving mother and father, but also because they had been warned by the doctors that he was inclined to be 'chesty'. Though by now he had grown out of his youthful weaknesses, he suffered a good deal at that time from colds, which generally went to his ears or chest. Mary Beck remembers that he was always having pink ears; and in due course he contracted, as Mrs. Beck put it, 'all the spotty diseases'. The Queen, who tries hard not to be a fussy mother, accepted these childish ailments as the inevitable fate of small boys at preparatory schools (though when he went down with measles in February 1961 the headmaster felt he must send daily bulletins by cable to Pakistan, where she and the Duke of Edinburgh were paying a state visit).

There was scope at Cheam for all the regular outdoor games and sports except riding. But Charles was frequently enough in the saddle at Sandringham and Balmoral. He had even, early in 1959, been taken on his pony to a meet of the West Norfolk Foxhounds. This had drawn down upon his parents a solemn rebuke from the National Society for the Abolition of Cruel Sports, and an equally solemn reply in a leading article in *The Times*: 'Why should the abolitionists arrogate to themselves the duty of instructing the Queen on how to bring up her children?' There would have been a great deal more indignation if publicity had been given to the fact that the Prince of Wales had already shed blood: the previous August at Balmoral he had been trusted with a gun and had brought home his first grouse for the cooking pot in the Castle kitchen.

At Cheam, however, his most lethal weapon was still the red water-pistol in the shrubbery. The outdoor sport in which the Prince most frequently shone was swimming. In team games he was only moderately successful, despite the fact that, according to Peter Beck, the school at that time was distinctly lacking in talent. In cricket he occasionally played for the first eleven, but his regular place was in the second. He made few runs and the team lost most of its matches, in spite of the gallant performance of his friend Mary Beck as wicket-keeper. He was a good deal better at football. He played and enjoyed both games, but preferred soccer to rugger, where, he complained, 'they always put me in the second row—the worst place in the scrum'. At soccer he rose in his last year to the dignity of captain of the First XI. Unhappily, this was the season in which Cheam lost every match.

He liked running but was not distinguished at it. Neither was his sister, who came every year to the school sports and ran in the visitors' race, but was never placed. It was generally felt, however, that she did her brother credit by the punctiliousness with which she always said 'Goodbye, sir' to the headmasters when she left. The Queen came over from Windsor or London about three times a term, which was the average for visits by parents. The Duke of Edinburgh came rather more often, and the Queen Mother paid a couple of visits. As at Hill House, the Queen brought no attendants and was treated, by her own request, with the minimum of ceremony. The only special arrangement made for her visits was that all those present, masters, boys and other visitors, were asked not to use a camera. Apart from this the Queen expected to be, and was, treated as 'just another Mum'; she arrived by car, driving herself, and after changing her shoes and getting out, was left to spend the afternoon entirely as she wished—which often meant going off into the woods to picnic with Charles and Anne. It is David Munir's opinion that she can never have felt more at home than she did at Cheam.

Peter Beck gives high credit to his boys for the loyalty with which they rallied round to protect their schoolfellow from publicity. The defences were very rarely penetrated. Mary Beck, practising the piano one night in her mother's drawing-room, heard some strange noise outside and saw red lights flashing like fireworks up and down the garden. An intruder was subsequently captured apparently trying to take photographs in the dark, but no camera was found on him.

A more serious alarm was raised in November 1959, when additional police were posted by the Chief Constable of Berkshire round the school. The danger ostensibly feared was an invasion of photographers for the Prince's approaching eleventh birthday; but it is believed that warning had been received of a possible Irish attempt to kidnap the Prince of Wales and hold him as hostage for the end of Partition. The Irish Republican Army denied knowledge of any such plot, and can probably be acquitted of complicity; but more serious suspicion attached at the time to a body of breakaway gunmen who called themselves Fianna Uladh, or 'Warriors of Ulster'.

After the first term it was not thought necessary to have a detective permanently resident in the cottage, though he was on duty when the Prince left the school precincts to play in a match, or to attend service at the village church at Headley. It was during one of these weekend tours of duty that the detective, Donald Green, knocked up the headmaster in the middle of the night to report that he had seen a mysterious figure prowling on the roof. The whole school was immediately roused. The roof was searched, but no conspirator found. Then the dormitories were also searched, and heads counted. But no boy was missing. The school, mystified, went back to sleep. Long afterwards a boy named Daukes confessed that he had only just managed to get back to bed with the skin of his teeth before the search party reached his dormitory, and lay stuffing a blanket in his mouth to muffle the sound of panting brought on by his hasty scramble across the tiles.

Between terms at Cheam the Prince continued to follow the usual holiday round of the four royal houses. At Easter 1959 Michael Farebrother came back as holiday tutor; and at Balmoral later that year Jean Lajeunesse of the French Canadian 22nd Regiment, the famous 'Vandoos', who was a graduate of the University of Montreal, was brought in to improve his French. When the family was at Buckingham Palace, Miss Peebles continued to take Charles and Anne on semi-educational visits, which ranged from the Battersea Fun Fair to Westminster Abbey and the London Planetarium to the Houses of Parliament and Scotland Yard, where the Prince was allowed to work the police wireless communication system, and called a radio car to pick the party up and drive them home. They visited Podrecca's Piccoli Theatre at the Victoria Palace, theoretically incogniti, and at the end of the performance took refuge from the crowd by going behind, where the Prince was shown how to work the marionettes he had been watching from the stalls. His great interest in animals led him several times to Regent's Park (he became a member of the Young Zoologists' Club, which is the junior branch of the Zoological Society of London). And in August 1960, this time with his mother and father, for the first time he attended a national festival of his own Principality—the Eisteddfod.

The part played by Miss Peebles in the Prince's life was rapidly decreasing and that of the Duke of Edinburgh growing greater. Father and son have always been very close together, and grew closer still as the boy reached an age to take part in adult sports. He was not by any means growing away from Princess Anne, who loved to share in all she could of his life and is much the more self-assertive character of the two; but on the moors or in the saddle it was becoming more difficult for her to keep up the pace. Nearly all the skill he acquired, out of school, in bodily exercises was taught him by his father—except for skating, which he learned at the Richmond stadium from Miss Betty Callaway, the professional instructress. After his first successful shot at a grouse at the age of ten, he was often with his father at the butts, and by the Christmas following his thirteenth birthday could be a recognized member of the shooting party and contribute a respectable number of pheasants to the game book at Sandringham. The Duke then introduced him to the internal combustion engine, and by the time he was twelve he was habitually driving a Land Rover on the private roads at Birkhall, though it was not until April 1967 that he successfully took the driving test and could show himself on the highway. He loved watching his father play polo, and clamoured to play himself. The Duke of Edinburgh, who had taken up the game at the time of his marriage in order to share in his bride's deep interest in horses and had since become an enthusiast, thought him too young to take part in a match, but spent a good deal of time with him on the practice grounds, teaching him the elements of pony control and the art of hitting the ball.

As might have been expected from the Duke of Edinburgh's naval background he was especially keen to interest Charles in water sports. During the Christmas holiday of 1958–9 they went off together from Sandringham to Hickling Broad for the annual coot shoot. The Norfolk Naturalists' Trust had lent them a bungalow; but when they got to Hickling they found it was flooded, so they put up at the Pleasure Boat Inn (where Mrs. Amis, the landlord's wife, met the emergency by the simple expedient of sending down to the village for Mrs. Mudd, who 'helps me out when I'm busy').

Shooting duck from a punt on the Broads does not call for the finer shades of watermanship. The following autumn the Prince of Wales began a more serious education in sail by going out with his father in a catamaran on Loch Muick; and the following June the GP Fourteenth Class Association presented the Duke with a fourteen-foot dinghy for the use of the Prince when he was old enough. This craft was lent, meanwhile, to the Central Council of Physical Education, to be used at their training centre on Windermere; and it appears to be still in their possession. The Prince has never been bitten with the itch to sail, as he has with the itch to shoot and play polo. At sea, he is content with modest semi-skilled work as a member of his father's crew. In most of his summer holidays from school he has sailed with his father round the fleet at Cowes; but after the early voyage to Tobruk his longest spells at sea before 1966 were two cruises of a week each in *Bloodhound* on the west coast of Scotland.

The Prince is keener than his father on fishing, though it was the Duke who first taught him. Later he learned from Rear-Admiral Christopher Bonham-Carter, Treasurer to the Duke, who fishes on the River Spey, and became highly skilled at fly-fishing for salmon. The more delicate dry-fly-fishing for trout he has not yet been able to practise, since the season, from May to June, exactly coincided with the summer term at school. With Admiral Bonham-Carter he once stayed for two nights at a village inn while on a fishing expedition. As he was packing his bags to leave, the Prince looked up and asked Bonham-Carter: 'Oughtn't I to go and say goodbye to the landlady?' It stuck in the Admiral's memory as one of many examples of the spontaneous good manners and consideration that are second nature to Prince Charles.

His progress through 'the spotty diseases' at Cheam had so far caused no great concern—except perhaps to his sister, to whom he passed on chicken pox at Easter 1959; but in February 1962 he woke up in the dormitory on a Sunday morning with alarming pains in his stomach. The school doctor, Basil Phillips, examined him and then telephoned for Sir Wilfred Sheldon, the Queen's Physician-Paediatrician, who hurried over by car and confirmed Phillips's diagnosis of appendicitis. He telephoned the Queen at Windsor and advised an immediate operation, to which she consented and a cable was sent to the Duke, who was on a visit to Venezuela. The Prince was driven by ambulance from Cheam to the Children's Hospital in Great Ormond Street, where the operation was performed in the small hours of Monday morning by the resident surgeon, David Waterson. He was taken from the operating theatre to a private ward, where four nursing sisters were on duty in rotation.

There was a time when appendicitis was a deadly menace. The Prince's ancestor, King John, probably died of it. Even in the early years of this century the operation was generally followed by six weeks or so in bed, much of the time in considerable discomfort. But recent advances in surgery have reduced the process to little more than a routine. Within a few days the Prince of Wales could sit up in bed and watch television on the set that had been installed in his room; he could talk to his mother by telephone between her visits, and even to his father in South America. Most of the Royal Family, including his grandmother and his sister and brother, came to see him; and one week after the operation he was able to entertain quite an international party, consisting of his cousins Princess Alexandra and Prince Michael of Kent, Princess Sophia and Princess Irene of the Hellenes, and Don Juan Carlos, the Spanish prince who was then engaged to (and has since married) Princess Sophia.

On the eleventh day after the operation he left hospital for convalescence at Windsor, and within a week he was fit to discharge the most grown-up function that had yet appeared on his programme. This was at one of the Queen's informal luncheon parties at Buckingham Palace: in the absence of her Consort abroad she asked her son to take his place as host. The Prince, now thirteen years old, proved himself quite able to hold his own in conversation with the varied company—about a dozen strong—which included a choreographer, a trade union leader, and the chairman of the B.B.C. It was one of the occasions that brought out the breadth of interests which so impressed Colonel Miller whose close contact with the Prince (he had been appointed Crown Equerry the previous year) began about this time.

The following day, March 1, the Prince felt robust enough to go skating at Richmond with his instructress, Betty Callaway; and on the eleventh he was back at school for the few weeks that remained of term.

In the Easter holidays, the day after being entertained at the White City television centre, where he watched 'Z Cars' in production, the Prince of Wales set off on his first visit to his father's branch of the family. All three of the Duke of Edinburgh's sisters, much older than himself, had been married before the war to German princes; and there had been an inevitably long period of broken contacts. Even now the connexion was looked on a little askance by many people in England, and the Duke's natural efforts in peacetime to keep in touch with his blood relations had to be conducted with considerable tact. But by this time, with the British Army settled on the Rhine as protector rather than conqueror of the new Western Germany, reconciliation was in the air; and the Queen as well as the Duke of Edinburgh thought it was time their son got to know his German cousins. There are seventeen of them in his generation, for all three of his aunts have large families. So, in his last holiday from Cheam, he made a start by going with his father to stay at Hesse, where his aunt Sophie lives, though her first husband, Prince Christopher of Hesse, was killed in 1944, and she has since married Prince George of Hanover. Here Charles renewed acquaintance with a son of the second marriage, Guelf, two years his senior, who had been a guest at Balmoral, and was shortly to be sent to school in Scotland. Father and son went on to visit another of the young Prince's aunts, Theodora Margravine of Baden and her three children, with whom, though at that time he spoke no German, he was soon on friendly terms. The whole expedition lasted only a little over a week, and they were home in time for the Ascot Gymkhana on April 22, where the Prince of Wales, on Bandit, tied with four other competitors for first place in a contest for ponies of 13·2 hands and under.

The Prince of Wales did not return to Cheam that summer. He had reached the rank of monitor and displayed his artistic talent at successive school exhibitions, in singing, and in the memorable performance as King Richard Crouchback. The dramatic critic of the *Cheam School Chronicle* had written: 'Prince Charles played the traditional Gloucester with competence and depth: he had a good voice and excellent elocution, and very well conveyed the ambition and bitterness of the twisted hunchback.' This favourable notice perhaps sweetened the pill administered by the football correspondent. Commenting in the same issue on that disastrous season of his captaincy, during which four goals were scored by Cheam and eighty-two by its opponents: 'At half, Prince Charles seldom drove himself as hard as his ability and position demanded.'

The men who had shaped this last phase of childhood felt that the Prince did them credit. He had never given them any trouble; he had come from a world neither they nor his schoolfellows knew, and had tried hard and successfully to leave all that out of his school life and become fully one of them. They remembered him as fundamentally good, though never a prig. He was outstanding in his consideration for other people: open-hearted and incapable of malice. In scholarship he was a conscientious all-rounder with no conspicuous weak spot anywhere (except perhaps those confounded figures). He left Cheam as very much a person; and in achieving personality he had not needed to draw upon the accidental advantage—if it is an advantage—that he was also a Prince.

## { 4 }

# IN FATHER'S FOOTSTEPS

M OST preparatory schoolboys leave for a public school
between the ages of thirteen and fourteen. The
Prince of Wales's thirteenth birthday fell on November 14,
1961; and by then it was clear that a decision must be taken
very soon about the next stage of his education. The Queen's
guiding principles continued to be: first, that we have a
good system of education in Great Britain, and the monarchy, as the supremely representative institution, should
take advantage of it; secondly, if her son was not educated
like other boys of his age, he would never in later life be
able to make the contact with his people which is necessary
for a King.

But these principles do not go far to help in choosing
between one school and another. A few voices were again
raised, urging that the Prince should be sent to one of the
state day schools in which the majority of his future subjects
are taught. In changing times it is possible that this will seem
the natural choice when he himself has to consider the upbringing of his children or grandchildren. But the objections
to it in present circumstances (outlined in a previous chapter) were reinforced by the consideration that the general

[ 81 ]

course of his education was predetermined when he was sent to Cheam, or even to Hill House. They prepare their pupils explicitly for the public schools, and it would be impracticable now to enter a different stream midway along its course—not that any of the Royal Family or their friends would have wished for such a sharp deflection.

But public schools today are more varied than they have ever been before and it was by no means necessary to choose one of the more conventional type. The Queen frankly recognizes that the whole world of school, and especially of boys' schools, is a mystery to her: she was content, like most mothers, to be guided in the main by her husband. Prince Charles himself was encouraged to give his own views, but naturally had little preference to express. He was not greatly looking forward to the imminent change of scene. Probably the majority of schoolboys at all times have thought of education as something at best tedious, if not positively unpleasant, to be got through; and the Queen knew that his first years at Cheam had been a misery to him. Only when the end was in sight did he begin to find happiness away from home; and now the prospect before him was of transfer to another strange environment, where there was no reason to suppose that life would be more enjoyable.

He was glad to be consulted, but he could not know what any public school was like until he got there. His name had been put down at birth for Eton—in case when the time came that should be the choice. But he did not think Eton sounded very attractive, mainly because it was in a town. It was of course the nearest school to home: just over the bridge from Windsor; but the Queen ruled out Eton for that very reason. He would be watched there all the time by the ubiquitous reporters and photographers, who would leave him little chance to get on with his education. She could not think of letting him go to any school 'on the milk run'. If anything, Prince Charles had a slight leaning towards

*Above:* Learning to paint at Windsor, 1956
*Below:* Shrimping with Alec Rankin, 1956
*Previous page:* Balmoral, 1956

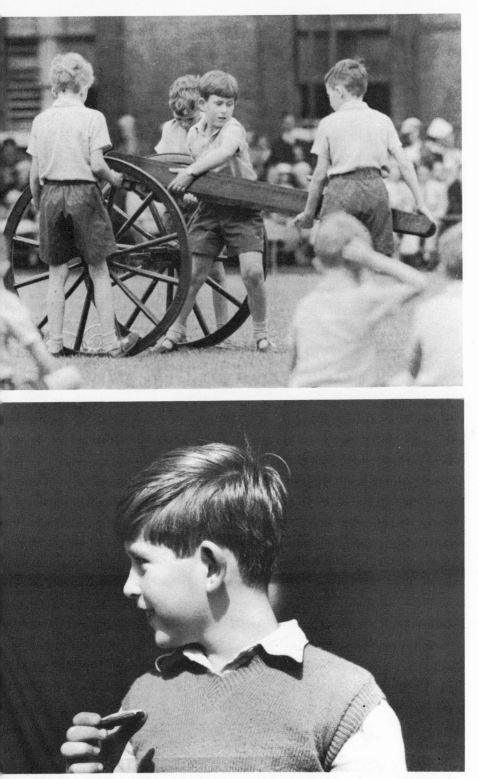

*Above:* Hill House Field Day, July 1957: dismantling a cannon
*Below:* A biscuit after a shooting lunch, 1958

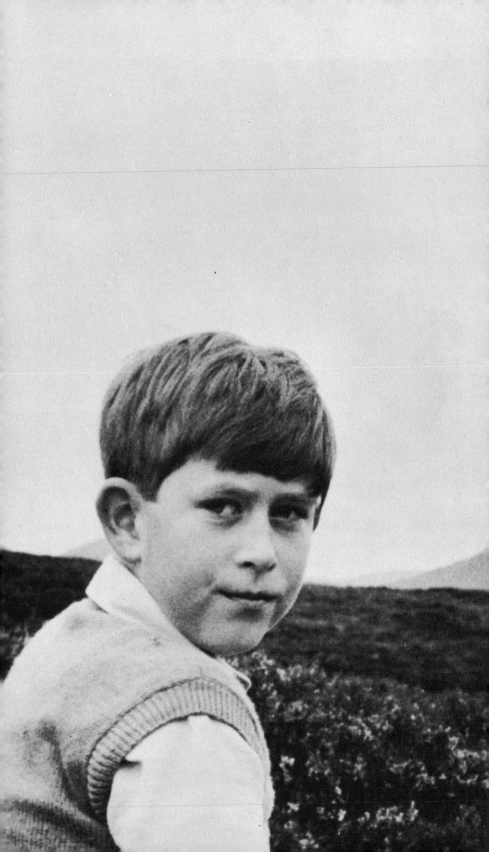

*Above:* Antony Armstrong Jones (now Lord Snowdon)
demonstrates the re-loading of a camera, 1959
*Opposite:* The Prince of Wales as a civil servant in the
film that never got made, 1959
*Previous page:* Mountain top near Balmoral, 1958
*Overleaf:* Labrador puppies, 1959

Charterhouse, where some of his friends from Cheam had gone. But the Duke of Edinburgh pressed the advantage of breaking out of the narrow circle of the ancient foundations.

A principal function of the monarchy to which Prince Charles is heir is to stand for continuity, to link the past with the future of the people, its traditions with its aspirations. Even at thirteen it was already apparent that his first sympathy was with tradition. His father, emphatically the most forward-looking of the family, was strongly in favour of a school whose bias should be towards the future. Moreover, the boy was of a shy and reticent disposition; something that would draw him out and develop a little more self-assertiveness in him seemed to be required. These were reputed to be the outstanding characteristics of Prince Philip's own old school at Gordonstoun. He himself had been very happy there, and he thought it was the very place for his son.

Prince Charles thought the publicity for the place 'sounded pretty gruesome'. But he readily admitted that he knew as little about it as about Eton; and to Gordonstoun it was decided that he should go. In effect the decision meant an attempt to mould him in his father's image, to which, although there is profound affection and confidence between the two, he did not naturally approximate. Whether this was the most suitable course is a question on which those who have advised the Queen on his education are still divided.

Gordonstoun in practice turned out to be a good deal less gruesome than the Prince of Wales had been led to believe. Its regimen and atmosphere are tough; but that is quite a different thing from being harsh or brutal.

It was modelled on the school that Prince Max of Baden founded in his castle-monastery at Salem, on the northern shore of the Bodensee, in 1919. Prince Max had been the last Chancellor of the Hohenzollern Empire. He had been intimately involved in the bitterness of defeat and the almost total collapse of Germany that followed it. In setting up the school he told his teachers to 'Build up the imagination of the boy of decision and the will-power of the dreamer so that in future wise men will have the nerve to lead the way they have shown, and men of action will have the vision to imagine the consequences of their decisions.' He added that their duty was to 'Train soldiers who, at the same time, are lovers of peace.'

Prince Max died ten years later; and in 1933 the headmaster whom he had appointed, Kurt Hahn, was driven from Germany because he was a Jew and because he had actively resisted the Nazis. Staying with a friend in Scotland, Hahn came upon the Gordonstoun estate near Elgin and decided that here was an ideal place to set up a school and carry on the work that was being increasingly impeded by the government in Germany. He took a lease on the seventeenth-century house and 300 acres of land and in the summer term of 1934 opened the school with three boys and and handful of masters—among them a young man named F. R. G. Chew who had spent four years teaching at Salem and was now to be in charge of climbing and sailing, as well as mathematics. Although the framework of daily life and the general method of education was to be the same as at Salem, Hahn was laying emphasis on a new purpose. 'I estimate,' he said, 'that about sixty per cent of boys have their vitality damaged under the conditions of modern boarding schools.' To counteract this he aimed 'to kindle on the threshold of puberty non-poisonous passions which act as guardians during the dangerous years'.

Dr. Hahn hoped to break the mould of an over-urbanized civilization by matching the physical energy of youth against real forces of nature on land and sea; at the same time giving them a sense of purpose by making at least a part of their training of benefit to their fellow-men. His aim was to strengthen simultaneously, and in harmony with one another, the mind, the body and the social conscience. There is nothing revolutionary in this. Some of the inspiration came from Eton. Very much the same line of thought had inspired Sir Robert Baden Powell in founding the Boy Scouts; the fundamental idea of the balanced man, fully developed in all his physical and intellectual capacities and dedicated to the common weal, is originally Athenian. Indeed, the fountain-head of all Dr. Hahn's educational thinking, and the work he most frequently quotes, is the *Republic* of Plato. The Duke of Edinburgh, who had been so completely at home at Gordonstoun and was its most famous old boy, was born a Greek Prince. The new boy of 1962 brought with him a historic motto—which his mother in her coming-of-age broadcast had hinted that she would like to have had for her own—'*Ich Dien*': 'I serve'.

The idea of public service is expressed in four highly organized units, staffed by the boys, two of them in direct connexion with official administration. One of these is the coastguard station, equipped with rockets and life-saving apparatus, which in stormy weather keeps a look-out for ships in distress. The other is the fire unit, trained under the supervision of professional firemen of the National Fire Service, and a fully recognized auxiliary. The mountain rescue unit has in its day actually saved lives. The fourth unit is trained to rescue swimmers.

The adventurous spirit is fostered by the cult of physical fitness and by far-ranging expeditions, by land and by water, which give the boys the self-reliance and self-control which the school motto, *Plus est en vous*, proclaims: it is a standing summons to keep muscle, mind and nerve always extended to the limit—the expanding limit—of natural capacity.

In 1936, two years after he had opened the school, Hahn introduced the Moray Badge, in conjunction with the Elgin Academy. The County Badge scheme grew from this. And these were evidently the inspiration for the Award Scheme later set up by the Duke of Edinburgh. It was Hahn who helped found the Outward Bound Sea School at Aberdovey in 1940 (when his own school had moved to Montgomeryshire for safety during the war), and later the Atlantic College scheme.

Kurt Hahn's ambitious ideals could be only dimly apprehended by the new boy who arrived, aged thirteen and a half, for the summer term of 1962. It was not his first sight of the buildings. Gordonstoun is easily accessible from Balmoral, and he had been over with his parents for a preliminary view, 'before being incarcerated', as he puts it. But the impression he then derived, even supplementing what his father had told him about the school, was very different from the institution as he learned to know it from the inside.

The Duke of Edinburgh drove him to Gordonstoun on the opening day. The road to the school branches off to the right from the Elgin-Duffus highway and leads through trees and beside playing fields to the old house, a handsome mansion with pepper-pot turrets and a fine balustraded roof to the middle section which was rebuilt in the eighteenth century and almost totally gutted by fire when troops were stationed there during the last war. To one side stands the Round Square, a great circular stable block enclosing a green lawn. Here one of the lairds was said to have dealings with the Devil. Today it is one of the school houses and the theatre in which open-air performances are given. Facing it is one of the four pigeon cotes built by the laird in the belief that if a man keeps pigeons his wife will soon die. With your back to the house you face a gentle hill rising to the skyline, and on the other side of the hill lies the sea. By a strange irony, all this estate was, until 1947, when the lease came to an end and the school bought it, the property of the Gordon-Cumming family. This same house was the home

of Sir William Gordon-Cumming, Lieutenant-Colonel of the
Scots Guards, whose career crashed in ruins after the Tranby
Croft scandal—the baccarat game in which a previous Prince
of Wales, Prince Charles's great-great-grand-father, had
dealt the hands and, in the view of the jury which tried the
subsequent libel action, Gordon-Cumming had cheated.

They were received by the headmaster, Mr. F. R. G.
Chew, who had taken over on Dr. Hahn's retirement,
accompanied by the Chairman of the Governing Body,
Captain Iain Tennant, the Warden, Mr. Henry Brereton,
and Peter Pace the Guardian, which is the title that Gordonstoun gives to its head boy and which Prince Philip held in
1938-9. This degree of ceremony was the due of the Queen's
Consort: it was not intended as a compliment to the new
boy: as usual, his parents had given instructions that he was
to be treated in every respect as just one of the rank and file.
The only unusual occurrence had taken place during the
previous term, when Mr. Chew had travelled down to Cheam
to lunch with Mr. Beck and to learn something about
his new pupil—but the mission had been so discreetly conducted that no word of it reached the newspapers. Four
days earlier the Press Secretary at Buckingham Palace had
issued a more general appeal:

'When publicity was reduced at the end of the first term
at Cheam School, it became possible for the whole school to
function in the normal way and therefore the Prince of
Wales was able to receive a normal education. . . . For this
the Queen and the Duke of Edinburgh are grateful, and I
am asked to say that they hope that this happy state of
affairs may continue during the Prince of Wales's stay at
Gordonstoun. Her Majesty and His Royal Highness fully
understand the very natural interest in the Prince of Wales's
education, but they feel that he will only be able to derive
full benefit from his days at school if he is not made the
centre of special attention.'

The Duke of Edinburgh left after lunching with the headmaster, picked up his own aircraft at Lossiemouth and gave his son a farewell tilt of his wings as he flew back over Gordonstoun. Prince Charles was left at Windmill Lodge, the house to which he had been allotted, to face the considerable ordeal of adaptation to a wholly strange society. He found it, he remembers, even worse than it had been at Cheam. This is not surprising. There is no greater shock for a boy than the jolt which brings down the captain of the eleven at the preparatory school to the insignificant status of a new boy once again. If he happens also to be rather shy by nature, the secret agonies he endures remain in his memory for years afterwards.

Windmill Lodge, a long, low, stone and timber building with a green asbestos roof, stands about a quarter of a mile from Gordonstoun House. The dormitories were bleaker than any he had yet encountered: bare wooden floorboards, unpainted walls, naked electric light bulbs hanging from the ceiling, and no furniture except the beds. Clothes were changed and kept in the locker rooms; meals were taken in one of the dining rooms at Gordonstoun House, at a table shared with thirteen other boys; for private study there were huts to be shared closer at hand.

The Prince of Wales was quickly introduced to the principle of service: not outside, but inside the school. This is not fagging. Juniors do not work for the comfort of the prefects personally, but for the benefit of the community as a whole. They take turns in waiting at table; they weed the garden; they clean up the classrooms, besides making their own beds and cleaning their own shoes. One of them is detailed as 'waker', to call the rest at 6.45 a.m. The chore that fell to the Prince of Wales most often in his first term was emptying the dustbins: a joke that his housemaster also enjoyed playing on Prince Alexander of Yugoslavia. Prince Charles himself found it a most appropriate form of menial task to bring him down to earth with a crash!

As soon as they had been wakened, the boys paraded in the open air, dressed only in shorts and running shoes, for physical drill or a quick trot round the grounds, followed by a cold shower, 'to shake the sleep out of them'. Breakfast was at eight. Class work began at nine and lasted through the morning, though twice a week it was interrupted by another spell of physical exercise. The subjects taught had to be the same as in any other school since all the boys were due to sit for the General Certificate of Education. They were English, Latin and French; History and Geography; Mathematics and several varieties of Natural Science. The Prince of Wales still found mathematics his great stumbling block, and history his chief interest; his ability to write good and graphic English, on which Peter Beck of Cheam had complimented him, continued to develop; his French was well ahead of other boys of his age, and in Latin he made average progress. He did not learn Greek.[1]

1. The Headmaster issues the following official summary of the

DAILY ROUTINE

The programme for the day is the same in winter and summer, with only minor adaptations.

7.0 An easy run round the garden, followed by wash and cold shower.

8.15 Breakfast. Surgery as necessary.

8.55 Morning Prayers.

9.10 Classwork begins. There are five 40-minute periods in the morning but for every boy one of these, on several days in the week, is a training break (running, jumping, discus- and javelin-throwing, assault course, etc.), under the Physical Training Master.

1.20 Lunch. After lunch there is a rest period (20 minutes): music or reading aloud to boys relaxing on their backs.

2.30 Afternoon activities. On three days a week there are either games (rugger and hockey in winter: cricket, lawn tennis or athletics in summer), or seamanship, or practical work on the estate. The proportion of time spent on each depends upon a boy's interests and development. One afternoon a week is allocated to the Services: Coast Guard Watchers, Sea Cadets, Army Cadets, Scouts, Fire Service, Mountain Rescue and Surf Life Saving. One afternoon and evening a week are

These lessons were continued for a couple of hours in the late afternoons (with two half-holidays in the week), supplemented by 'preparation' in the evening, at first in the junior common room, and after the first year in Prince Charles's share of the study to which he was presently promoted. It was in the afternoon activities that Gordonstoun expressed its individuality.

When not otherwise engaged the boys were allowed almost unfettered freedom to range about the country and the shore, although the town of Elgin was out of bounds; and the Prince of Wales made acquaintance with a number of the country people living in the neighbourhood. But the times for being 'not otherwise engaged' were limited. Most of the usual games were included in the curriculum—cricket, football, hockey, lawn tennis. The Prince took his part in them all, without any conspicuous success. He had captained the first eleven at Association football at Cheam; but the football played at Gordonstoun was Rugby, a game he never learned to enjoy. But he had played under both codes at Cheam, and his distaste for Rugby did not prevent his selection to play in his first winter term for the Junior Colts against an Aberdeen fifteen on the home ground. At that early stage any hope he may have once nourished of shining in school games seems to have petered out. His interests lay elsewhere. He had no desire to be in a team because on Saturdays he was usually longing to go out with some of the people he had met in the district. It was another manifestation of a familiar trait in his character. He has a great gift for

given to work on boys' individual projects which are exhibited and judged at the end of each year. On Saturday afternoons there are matches and opportunities for expeditions. Each boy with Training Plan has one free afternoon a week.

4.0 Warm wash and cold shower. Change into evening school uniform. Tea. After tea, two classes or tutorial periods.

6.20 Supper, followed by preparation in Houses or by 'Societies'.

9.15 Bedtime; silence period of five minutes.

9.30 Lights out. (There are some modifications for juniors.)

getting on well with people—people much older than himself, people even younger, people of all classes and conditions. But he feels no special preference for the society of his own age and his own kind, and the idea of being absorbed into cliques, groups or teams with them has no natural appeal. He is sociable, but not gregarious.

The lack of ambition or ability to excel in organized games did not count against Prince Charles in public opinion as it might have done at a more conventional school. Gordonstoun has never encouraged hero-worship of the athlete, preferring to exalt activities more closely related to real life. It sees a better training ground in the mountains and the sea, a better testing ground for the qualities of determination, of resource, of self-reliance, by which it sets most store. Many of the masters and boys would say that it is mastery of the sea that they admire most of all. Training *through* the sea is the characteristic Gordonstoun activity and is required of all. Training *for* the sea, the subject of the nautical course, is for specialists, of whom Prince Charles is not one. 'The little harbour of Hopeman, two miles from the school,' writes the Warden, 'is our best playing field.'

The Prince of Wales, having had the run of his father's yachts at Cowes and in coastwise cruises to the North, was past the elementary stages of seamanship, although he remained more at home in the water than upon it. Thanks to his early instruction in the pool at Buckingham Palace, even before he entered Hill House, he was able to swim like a fish. At Gordonstoun he took to the water at once. He formed a partnership with his cousin Guelf, and they qualified together to receive certificates of proficiency in life-saving on Charles's fourteenth birthday. The test for this was carried out in the indoor baths at Elgin; but he also swam in the sea and practised surf-riding beneath the cliffs of Morayshire. This was a sport that particularly attracted him, and he was disappointed some years later in missing the opportunity to practise it among the acknowledged masters of the art in New South Wales. However, he was qualified to take his place in the surf-rescue unit in which the school took pride, and to that extent had early gained status among the juniors of Gordonstoun.

Before that, in his first term, he took part in one of the most strenuous of the Gordonstoun exercises, an expedition by canoe from Hopeman Beach to Findhorn Bay. The distance between the two is about twelve miles as the crow flies, but allowing for wind and current the party covered well over the twenty-four miles before they reached home again. On the way the wind rose and with it the sea. The Prince of Wales was practically in a state of collapse when he reached the shore, but strengthened in self-reliance and self-esteem. The voyage had taken up the whole day. As he looks back on it today, he regrets that he never had the time to repeat the adventure.

He went home to Sandringham for the Christmas holidays with a new sense of dignity at having overcome difficulties by his own efforts. He had not enjoyed his first two terms: looking back today he feels he cannot honestly use the word 'enjoyment' about any stage of school life before the final phase. But he had found his feet among his schoolfellows; he knew that he was respected for himself and not for his royal rank; and he could face with a new self-confidence any challenge in the future.

At the beginning of the New Year, 1963, not accompanied this time by any of his English family, he was off to Bavaria, to visit his uncle, Prince Georg Wilhelm of Hanover, and his aunt, Sophie, *en route* for a winter-sports holiday in the Engadine. This was his first opportunity to learn to ski, and he plunged into the new experience with enthusiasm. Unhappily, the old trouble recurred: crowds of reporters, photographers and curious spectators dogged the beginner's halting footsteps in the snow, so that for most of

his short holiday he had to confine himself to the slopes
within the private property of his host, Prince Ludwig of
Hesse; and even there he needed a protective guard of Swiss
police, themselves patrolling on skis. Still, he learned enough
to be able to improve by practice when the snow fell in the
Morayshire mountains or the hills behind Balmoral. On the
way home he was able to pay a fleeting visit to his uncle the
Margrave Berthold of Baden at Salem Castle—the same
Salem which was the birthplace of Gordonstoun.

The completion of his first year at Gordonstoun was
followed by two new accessions of dignity. The first was
when the Queen directed the Kings of Arms to register her
son's armorial 'achievement'. This consists basically of her
own shield showing the four quarters of England, Scotland,
Ireland and England again, supported by the English lion
and the Scottish unicorn, surmounted by the crest of the
crowned lion and encircled with the blue garter inscribed
'*Honi Soit Qui Mal Y Pense*'. For the Prince the shield, sup-
porters and crest are all 'differenced' with a label, that is, a
plain white or silver riband with three pendants, denoting
the eldest son. In the middle of the great shield is set a
smaller one, an 'escutcheon of pretence', having over it the
heir apparent's coronet and showing the quarterly red and
gold with four leopards counterchanged of Llewelyn the
Great and the native Princes of Wales. In place of the
Queen's motto, '*Dieu Et Mon Droit*' appears the Prince's own
'*Ich Dien*'.[1] For use in Scotland it is the Scottish quarter of
the shield that takes precedence and is repeated, the unicorn
exchanges with the lion in the place of honour on the
'dexter' side, and the lion of the crest is in the Scottish sitting
pose, holding a sword and a sceptre.

All this was borne by the last Prince of Wales, Edward,
now Duke of Windsor. An innovation was made for Prince

1. 'The heir, as long as he is a child, differeth nothing from a servant.'
Galatians iv, 1.

Charles by adding under the shield and between two roundels containing the heir apparent's feathers and Welsh dragon, a third showing the fifteen besants, or gold pieces, of the Duchy of Cornwall. (They are believed to have originated as green peas, alluding to the fact that the first royal Earl of Cornwall, Richard, brother of Henry III, had been Count of Poix in Normandy.) The arms on this shield will when occasion arises be displayed on the Prince's banner which will fly over his home when he is in residence, and hang over his stall in the Garter Chapel of St. George.

To the fourteen-year-old schoolboy, however, returning to Gordonstoun in May to begin his second year, the acquisition of this emblazoned splendour was of less practical account than the second mark of enhanced dignity: his enrolment in the 'Junior Training Plan'.

This was a recognition that he had passed out of the probationary phase. It meant release from the closer forms of supervision, and the assumption of a growing degree of responsibility for the regulation of his own life. He could choose more freely among the various forms of out-of-class activity that Gordonstoun offered. At the same time he was required to make a kind of examination of conscience every evening, and write down the results in a manuscript book made out for the purpose. He was to state what he had done to justify his existence or advance his progress towards the all-round excellence of the school ideal; what expeditions he had joined in, what jobs he had done for the service of the school community or for the world outside; and he was to confess in writing all the day's backsliding.

This confession is not confined to breaches of the school rules, or failure to perform any of the routine duties and disciplines of the day: it extends to the recording of any surrender to personal bad habits, such as wool-gathering in class or over-indulgence in sweets. The statements made in the book are not checked, for the foundation of the Gordons-

[ 94 ]

toun system is trust; and when truthfulness is made a matter of honour very few boys, and certainly not Prince Charles, would betray that trust. Being, as all who know him agree, an exceptionally conscientious boy, and a naturally introvert character, he was likely to find this habit of self-judgment comparatively easy to acquire; on the other hand, the obligation to write down his findings was bound to be more distasteful to him than to less sensitive natures. He was proud of the mark of trust bestowed upon him, and the Junior Training Plan undoubtedly raised his self-confidence; but it did not make school life any easier.[1] Its only immediate effect was that, in accordance with Gordonstoun tradition, he was grabbed, hustled along to the showers and ducked.

The ordeal of the canoeing expedition to Findhorn Bay had not weakened his determination to master the sea. In his second term he qualified for inclusion in one of the crews that replaced each other in succession on one or other of the two school ketches that sailed round the northern coast. Charles was posted to the *Pinta* and was on board when the ship arrived at Stornoway, on the Isle of Lewis, on Monday, June 17. He and four other boys were given leave to have lunch ashore and then go to the cinema; as usual, they were accompanied by the Prince's private detective, Donald Green, who had gone to Gordonstoun with him and was normally accommodated in the masters' quarters. As they walked to the Crown Hotel, it was soon evident that some of the people in Stornoway had recognized the Gordonstoun boat and had come along to see if the Prince was on board. By the time the detective led them into the lounge

1. The ladder of promotion at Gordonstoun is rather complicated, and has many rungs: School Uniform, Junior Training Plan, Senior Training Plan, White Stripe, Colour Bearer Candidate. At the top there are also Captains and their Assistants and above them all the Guardian. Some of the steps depend on the votes of the boys themselves. Prince Charles got his School Uniform in his first term and eventually climbed all the way.

of the Crown, there was a small crowd forming outside.

Donald Green went off to the cinema to book seats; the boys waited in the hotel lounge for him to come back and join them for lunch. Meanwhile, the people outside continued to peer in and the Prince, who hates being treated as a peep-show, particularly when it looks like making him ridiculous in front of his schoolfellows, grew more embarrassed and fidgety. He recalls that he got 'absolutely fed up' and took refuge in the next room of the hotel, where he could no longer be stared at from outside. But the next room turned out to be a bar, with a row of people sitting on stools and presently looking rather inquiringly at him. He realized that this was a place where one was expected to order a drink or go away; and having realized this he became acutely embarrassed and at a loss for what to do. He was certainly aware that a fourteen-year-old boy could not drink wine on licensed premises without breaking the rules of Gordonstoun and the laws of the land. But he was not in a mental state to consider any of this at the moment. He stepped up to the bar and, recalling the drink that he had sometimes been given when out shooting at Sandringham, ordered cherry brandy. He paid his half-crown to the barmaid and then there walked in what he can still only think of as "that dreadful woman".

The dreadful woman was a freelance journalist. Other Gordonstoun boys on these sea trips were in the habit of taking a glass of something or other when they came ashore, and the practice was winked at. But the journalist had recognized this particular Gordonstoun boy and by next day the story had gone right round the world. The teetotallers of Scotland, and of England and Wales as well, were up in arms. On the Continent, where the smallest toddlers expect a glass of diluted wine with their dinner, there was mystification; the impression grew that the heir to the British Throne must have been discovered in a drunken orgy.

[ 96 ]

The uproar came as a sequel to several public criticisms of the Prince over the previous year. In September it had become known that he had shot his first stag on the hills above Balmoral, and the League against Cruel Sports, meeting at Caxton Hall, had passed a motion condemning this. In March Charles had been attacked by a minister of the Free Church of Scotland for 'invading the Lord's Day' with a party of other Gordonstoun boys, practising ski-ing in the Cairngorms on a Sunday. In May a Bill for the protection of deer had come before the House of Commons and in Standing Committee one member referred to 'the Duke of Edinburgh, who goes in for this loathsome kind of sport and even brings his child up to do it'.

To make matters worse, the newspaper reports of the Stornoway incident were followed by an official denial—based on a misunderstood telephone conversation with the Prince's detective. The denial was followed by confirmation of the original news story; and the confirmation was followed by a withdrawal of the denial: a series of mishaps that served to keep the episode alive longer than need be. It would no doubt have been given even more attention but for the fact that the Profumo affair, after simmering since March, had now come to the boil. Scandal will still sell more newspapers than Royalty—even than Royalty and Drink!

There was, of course, still the question of what punishment should follow the crime. The Stornoway police were reported to have served a summons on the hotel proprietor —and withdrawn it. *The Times* commented that the headmaster of Gordonstoun would investigate and, if necessary, award punishment: and that a cane was kept for that purpose.

On his return to school the Prince climbed the broad wooden staircase in the old house that leads to the headmaster's study: two lofty rooms made into one, the windows looking out at the back of the house over the long stretch of ornamental water and the avenue of chestnut trees. (And beside one of the windows, under an armchair, what the headmaster describes as 'a useful device for disposing of unruly boys'—a concealed trapdoor leading down to a hiding place probably constructed in the very early days when a Catholic family lived there.)

On Monday, June 24, Mr. Chew stated that 'the incident was closed', though he did not reveal in what fashion. In fact, the Prince was not beaten, though that was the atonement he would have much preferred. Instead his Junior Training Plan was revoked—he was reduced to the ranks. Though he resignedly set himself to win back his place, and succeeded by the end of the term, he had been hit harder than he could have been with the cane.

It had been a very trivial storm in a teacup, or liqueur glass, but it made a significant impression on the Prince of Wales. The Queen is able to smile at all the hubbub and thinks that in the end it did her son good. He learnt in 'the hard way' something of the restraints that his position must always place on even his most casual behaviour. The Prince himself tries to laugh at it, but still finds this difficult to do.[1] After the storm had blown up and before Charles had left Stornoway, some local wag came down to the quay and, pointing to the name *Pinta* on the bows of the ketch, shouted across: 'She'll belong to the Milk Marketing Board, no doubt?' It was years before the Prince could see anything funny in this.

There is a long tradition that the heir to the throne should have some experience in one of the armed services of the Crown and, willing as the Queen had been to let her son's education depart from old precedents, she and he are most

1. The injustice rankles. When he speaks of it, his eyes have a look of pain, even of repressed anger. I remember seeing the identical expression once before. It was on the features of George VI, when somebody made an indiscreet reference to one of the events in his life by which he had been most grievously hurt: the abdication of his brother Edward VIII. But this is comparing small griefs with great.

unlikely to set this tradition aside. The probability is that the Prince will wish to see something of more than one service. Gordonstoun maintains a Combined Cadet Force with military and naval sections, and he had training in both. He spent his first two years in the Army section, with the conventional routine of 'square-bashing', route marching, field days and so forth, acquiring on the way a reasonable measure of skill in map-reading, field-cookery and first aid. For the latter part of his schooldays he transferred to the naval section, where his training was supplemented by taking an active part in the school's coastguard unit. As a member of the naval section he went for a spell to H.M.S. *Vernon*, the Portsmouth training camp. He lived in barracks and underwent what the Queen thought the salutary experience of being roared at by petty officers; he had now enough resilience to take these formidable taskmasters in his stride. The training in H.M.S. *Vernon* is concerned with diving, torpedoes, anti-submarine tactics and minesweeping. The royal cadet's arrival had been kept secret at the Queen's desire; but even so the Navy thought it necessary for a bodyguard to follow him round Portsmouth harbour in a separate craft when he embarked on an exercise with a boarding party to scale the decks of a whaler. The Prince recalls those weeks as one of the most enjoyable times of his Gordonstoun years, much more enjoyable than his army training, and prides himself on having acquired a considerable understanding of anti-submarine warfare.

The Queen notices that the Prince of Wales is not great on hobbies; yet the word is as good as another to apply to a special interest which engaged his mind and his muscles for several terms and which he hopes to develop further. History had long been his favourite classroom subject; he now found himself caught by the spell of prehistory, the study of the remote past of humanity in the millennia before written records. The instrument of prehistory is archaeology, the unearthing and interpretation of the material relics that our inarticulate ancestors have left behind them; but its subject matter is closely akin to social anthropology, the study of the way of life of the multifarious races of man, living today or veiled in the mist of the ages. It was this aspect of archaeology that captured and still holds the imagination of the Prince of Wales.

He read up what could be found about the archaeology of Morayshire in the school library, and then went out with a digging party of Gordonstoun boys to look for evidence. In the course of several terms they dug many tons of earth out of a cave in the cliffs. They convinced themselves that by removing the accumulation of centuries they had reached a surface on which men and women had lived and left traces of their habitation: an 'occupation level'. Even if they were deluded, the Prince found it great fun and it gave him a lasting passion for archaeology.

The diggers even lit a fire on the level to see how the cavemen might have lived. But when the smoke became thick thousands of spiders dropped from the roofs and the Prince made a hurried exit!

The summer term of 1964, which followed his training in H.M.S. *Vernon*, was a time of anxiety and concentration for most of the boys of Prince Charles's year: at the end of it they were to sit for their O-level examination. In all subjects but two he had no reason to distrust his prospects: he was a steady worker and was amply prepared for the ordeal. When the time came he passed comfortably in Latin, French, history and English language and literature. But mathematics and physics were still the stumbling block. He had been grinding at them conscientiously, not to say painfully; but he lacked any sort of flair for the subject. He was not going to be defeated; he plodded for term after term; but it was not till December 1965 that he at last struggled through, when he was in the Senior Training Plan, had just been made a prefect, and was about to leave Gordonstoun, at any rate for a time.

At the end of that summer term, just after the examination, he was one of a party of Gordonstoun boys invited to go camping on the Balmoral estate. There he had the misfortune to contract pneumonia, and was hastily removed to the Watson-Fraser nursing home. It was the most serious illness he had yet suffered, and the Queen anxiously flew from London to his bedside. But within a fortnight he was able to be flown to Buckingham Palace and begin the holiday round at Cowes.

This year the end of the holiday was varied by a diversion farther afield than Balmoral. In September the Prince of Wales and his father, accompanied by Princess Anne, were invited to Athens to represent the British Royal Family at the wedding of the young King Constantine of the Hellenes to the Danish Princess Anne-Marie. This was quite an intimate family affair: the Duke of Edinburgh, who had been born a Prince of Greece and Denmark, was closely related to both bridegroom and bride. It was not the first time the brother and sister had been together on such an occasion, for the previous year the Prince of Wales had sat with his mother in Westminster Abbey while Princess Anne was principal bridesmaid at the marriage of their cousin Princess Alexandra to Angus Ogilvy. In Athens Princess Anne was again the chief of five bridesmaids but this time her brother had a part of his own to play. In the Greek wedding service gold crowns are held over the heads of both bride and bridegroom while parts of the liturgy are recited, the crownbearers usually taking turns to hold the crown because the strain is considerable. At the royal wedding Prince Charles was one of ten young men sharing this office. With his hand stretched high to hold the crown above the King's head he soon began to appreciate the need to distribute the labour among several sets of sinews: grit his teeth as he would, his arm began to flag, and the Queen Mother Frederika had to step forward to his aid.

The wedding festivities did not take up the whole of what turned out to be a very pleasant brief holiday in the golden Aegean sunshine; but the Prince again found that his leisure hours were invaded by the press. With Princess Anne, the Swedish Crown Prince Carl Gustaf and others of the younger guests at the wedding, including some of his German cousins, he was sunbathing on a raft at Vouliagmeni, near Athens. They were protected by Greek naval police, patrolling in paddle boats. But three French photographers managed to slip through this screen and approached the raft, from which several of the young princes launched a counter-attack.

What happened next is not altogether clear; but some of the French papers were ablaze the next day with indignation at the report that two of their innocent compatriots had been brutally ducked without provocation by sprigs of British and Swedish royalty. The two photographers certainly got very wet; but they had taken the risk with their eyes open: they were obviously trespassing and any young men, princes or peasants, might have retaliated in the same way.

If Prince Charles had given them their dowsing it would be easy to excuse him. The photographers had succeeded in boarding his raft. He had vivid memories of a recent unhappy encounter with the press. He had heard his father expressing forthright opinions about the photographers who hampered his sailing at Cowes. But in fact it was one of his cousins who got to them first, although he was very close. Whatever Charles's intentions may have been, the invaders had been repelled before he reached them. Although his cousin tipped them in, the Prince of Wales remembers that they facilitated their entry into the water by scrambling to the far side of the raft, which then decanted them into the sea. Their sufferings were not so terrible that they were unable to get their photographs into print. If Prince Charles was a little surprised by the wealth of dramatic detail in the stories that accompanied the pictures, he recognized that there was no malice in the incident. Unlike the cherry brandy affair, it left no rankling memories behind.

But he was scarcely back at Gordonstoun for the new term when he found himself in the news again—and this time in a particularly distasteful context. At the end of September, the exercise book in which he wrote his weekly essay disappeared in circumstances strongly suggesting that it had been stolen. There had been previous incidents to show that there was a market for such things. Once an exercise book purporting to contain the Prince's writings had been offered for sale but quickly found to be a forgery; another, retrieved from a master's waste-paper basket, was genuine, but the work of another boy. This time it was quickly realized that something authentic had got into the wrong hands—as Mr. Chew, the headmaster, told the police, it might be regarded as 'a collector's piece'.

Very soon it was discovered that the book was being hawked round the newspaper offices and press agencies—in fact two books seemed to be on offer, only one of which could be genuine. Eventually detectives from Scotland Yard ran the true book to earth in Lancashire and took possession; but the whole story blazed into publicity in November when, six weeks after the book was first missed, the Mercury Press of St. Helens issued a writ against the Metropolitan Police, claiming the return of 'goods wrongly taken'.

This was bluff. The essays were stolen property and could not possibly have become the lawful property of any receiver. But the seizure of the booty by the police was too late to undo the damage. It had certainly changed hands more than once in the course of the shady chaffering that had gone on; and at some stage or other photostat copies had presumably been made. It was no doubt one of those copies that had been sold abroad, enabling the German magazine *Der Stern* to publish a translation of the essays on November 17. No doubt proceedings might have been taken in the name of the Prince of Wales under the international copyright conventions; but the award of damages would be no compensation for the affront to British royalty. The Queen's Press Secretary issued a statement, reserving judgment on the genuineness of *Der Stern*'s version until a copy of the magazine should reach England, but meanwhile saying that it was 'highly regrettable that the private essay of a schoolboy should have been published at all in this way'.

It turned out that the authenticity of the essays could not be denied. There was nothing in them for the Prince to be ashamed of; on the other hand the opinions they contained were no more mature than would be expected of any boy of sixteen, and any such boy or his parents might resent their being blared about the world. The mischief had been done, and cannot be aggravated by the inclusion here of a few words about the contents of the book.

One of the essays, on the corrupting effects of power, was in fact not an expression of Prince Charles's views at all: it was a précis he had been told to make from a set book by the historian Lecky. Another exercise was to set down in ten minutes a list of the articles he would choose to have with him in the case of being wrecked on a desert island. His very practical selection was a tent, a knife, a portable radio (both for news and for the hope of rescue) and lots of rope and string.

Readers avid for a clue to the political opinions of a future King of England fastened on two of the essays. One of these was on democracy, and showed the Prince of Wales deploring the tendency to vote for a party rather than for the personality of the candidate. He thought it wrong that, for example, an unattractive Tory should get a vote because the elector happened to oppose the nationalization of steel or the abolition of the public schools. The second essay, on the press, might possibly have been expected to betray bias and a sense of persecution. But instead the Prince of Wales argued strongly for the full freedom of the press as an indispensable exposer and critic of the abuses of government. He added a good word for television as the most effective medium for keeping the young informed and stimulated.[1]

If *Der Stern* had done no more than give a wide circulation to these not very startling sentiments, the Prince would no doubt have been content to shrug the affair aside as a trivial exhibition of international bad manners. What he could not forgive, and has never forgiven, is the editor's gratuitous embellishment of the story: the Prince, it was alleged, running short of pocket-money, had raised the wind by selling his essays to another Gordonstoun boy for thirty shillings. Almost immediately the American magazine *Time* came forward with a highly circumstantial story, purporting to trace the commercial channels through which the book had reached the German periodical. To the charge against the Prince of having tried to turn his school writings into cash it added the further allegation that he had done much the same thing at Cheam by selling his autograph. It then proceeded to describe the profitable resale of the essay book by the original purchaser, and the way it passed at increasing prices through other hands until the time when *Der Stern* gave £1,000 for the first serial rights. Other sales were stated to have brought in a further £4,000. The article was published under the title, 'The Princely Pauper'.

It is very possible that the whole series of transactions after the first had been accurately uncovered and recorded. But the following issue of *Time* contained a letter from the

1. The Queen sees another side of the picture. She is glad to find her son getting fond of serious reading; but the taste has taken a long time to develop, and she thinks this is partly due to the distraction of the television screen.

Press Secretary: an indignant denial, very rare in the cautiously worded correspondence of the Household.

'There is no truth whatever,' Sir Richard Colville wrote, 'in the story that Prince Charles has sold his autograph at any time. There is also no truth whatever that he sold his composition book to a classmate. In the first place he is intelligent and old enough to realize how embarrassing this would turn out to be, and second he is only too conscious of the interest of the press in anything to do with himself and his family. The suggestion that his parents keep him so short of money that he has to find other means to raise it is also a complete invention. Finally, the police would not have attempted to regain the composition book unless they were quite satisfied that it had been obtained illegally.'

The sense of injustice engendered by this affair still brings a note of bitterness into Prince Charles's voice. He considers that he was most unfairly treated. It is not so much the imputation of mercenary conduct that he resents: what he cannot forgive is the implication that he used his position to give a factitious money value to writings which he quite realizes were immature and in themselves of no more interest than those of any other schoolboy. There was always the clearest understanding that all privileges of rank were suspended for the duration of his schooldays, and to trade upon them in any way would be utterly alien to his character.

The storm over the essay book rumbled on beyond the end of term, and was still audible when the Prince of Wales with Princess Anne went off, immediately after Christmas, for another winter sports holiday in Liechtenstein, as the guest of Prince Franz Josef and his wife, Princess Gina. His hostess was with him when he fell off a ski-lift, but the snow was soft and she reported no harm was done. There was the usual difficulty in dodging the press, but this time a gentlemen's agreement was concluded. If Prince Charles and Princess Anne were given their mornings in peace, the photographers would be welcome on the slopes in the afternoon. With this respite from disturbance the Prince of Wales, in spite of a tumble during a lesson in which he broke a ski, continued to make good progress.

He was also able to congratulate himself on a mild tactical victory. On New Year's Day in 1965 a procession of five cars left Vadus Castle. The first three dashed past the waiting photographers before the passengers could be identified; but there was no mistaking—indeed there was intended to be no mistake about—the drivers of the last two: they were the Duke of Edinburgh and Prince Franz Josef. The photographers promptly drove in pursuit; and when the two princes broke away from the procession by a side road they followed suit, confident that the British royal children must be in the back of one or the other car. In fact both were concealed in the first car of all, and gleefully celebrated their success in giving the combined 'enemy' forces the slip.

His father's opinion of some press tactics—the intrusive microphones, the cameramen who wouldn't take no for an answer—was well known. By now, Prince Charles had good reason to share them. He also had an unfortunate habit of scowling whenever press cameras were pointed at him, more from embarrassment than bad temper. Although he is better than average as an actor on the stage, it has taken him a long time to become accustomed to the harmless subterfuges and small hypocrisies of the royal profession: the ready smile, the suggestion that the person you are now talking to is the one you have been waiting all your life to meet. So that until very recently most press snapshots of him showed a frowning or deeply serious face that quite belied his very humorous and often high-spirited nature.

Back at Gordonstoun for the last unbroken year he would spend there, the Prince of Wales was finding school life growing rather more tolerable. He had a study to himself now. He had graduated to the Senior Training Plan, which is a stiffer version of the Junior, but leaves still more to the participant's self-discipline. He continued to play his part in team games, in projects and expeditions, accepting all the strains and challenges, but still without ambition to excel in games. The sports that really stirred him were those he could enjoy only in the holidays: field sports, which drew him as they did his mother and father and grandmother. 'The whole family,' says Miss Anderson, 'goes out in weather that most people would think mad. Last holidays he would be out shooting all day, then tea, then fishing in the evening.'

He had added polo to the *grandes passions* that Kurt Hahn was so anxious to inculcate in the growing boy. It was in August that year that he played for the Rangers in his first public tournament, and scored two goals. In comparison with this, Rugby football and cricket, dutifully played but at his own unassuming level, seemed tame. He was becoming steadily more conscious of the resources within himself on which he could draw, and through which his character was developing.

It was the all but invariable rule that no public ceremony was important enough to justify an interruption of the Prince's school life. But one exception was made early in this first term of 1965. He came south to sit silent with his parents in St. Paul's doing honour to the memory of Sir Winston Churchill at the State Funeral.

He was to be confirmed at Easter: the Archbishop of Canterbury was coming to Windsor to perform the ceremony. In preparation the Prince of Wales had been receiving instruction in the holidays from the Dean of Windsor, who found in him a natural affinity for the type of 'prayer-book' Anglicanism, remote from the extremes of either the High Church or the Low, to which the Queen and other members of the Royal Family adhere. In the Dean he found not solely a spiritual confidant but also an enthusiastic companion when he went rummaging over the remoter recesses of Windsor Castle, clambering up the remains of Henry II's palace to examine chimneys and mural decorations of the twelfth century, and generally indulging his passion for the past. With O-levels out of the way—except for the still unexorcized spectre of mathematics—he could afford to let his imagination range more widely over these congenial fields.

He had a natural capacity to appreciate not only literature, but all the arts, and had the ability to practise several of them. He knew at the same time that, in what Dr. Johnson called 'the tumultuary life of princes', there is no room to develop such talents beyond a very modest amateur level. But it was from these that he could for the present derive most satisfaction. He could not attempt everything: the strenuous life of Gordonstoun leaves even a senior boy limited leisure. At Hill House he had shown promise with pencil and brush, and at Cheam he had still delighted to draw and paint; at Gordonstoun he let this interest fall away.

But he did wish to continue some handiwork, and among the varieties offered at Gordonstoun, which included carpentry and metal work, his choice had early fallen on pottery. In this he attained some skill, and showed his ceramic products in school exhibitions.

Far more important was his developing taste and versatility in music. He had sung in the school choir at Cheam; after his voice broke he sang again in the bass chorus at Gordonstoun. His home environment was encouraging, for both his mother and his grandmother were music-lovers, and the talent of his aunt, Princess Margaret, for light-hearted improvisation on the piano is well known. The first instrument he attempted was the piano; but he confesses that his progress with this was hampered by his inability to read two lines of music at once. At Gordonstoun he turned to the trumpet as a more single-minded sort of instrument, and was soon playing it successfully in school concerts and in public performances in several parts of Scotland. In a recital of religious music in St. Giles Cathedral, Edinburgh, he doubled the parts of trumpeter in the orchestra and singer in the choir. He thoroughly enjoys making music with his lungs, and trumpet pieces are still in his repertory; but a new musical world opened to him in his later days at Gordonstoun when he began to play the 'cello. This instrument is his latest love, and, to judge by the enthusiasm with which he speaks of it, probably his last. He finds it the most beautifully sensitive instrument he knows, with marvellous tone variations and depth of sound, although under his own bow he fears it sounds like the squeaking of an old church door—an excessively modest estimate that is not borne out by the conductors who have heard him play. At a second recital in St. Giles he played both the trumpet and the 'cello; and in a concert in Elgin Town Hall he played Schubert, Mozart and Rossini. He remembers this as an outstandingly wonderful experience. One feels, as his eyes light up with enthusiasm, that his 'cello gave him the purest pleasure he knew at Gordonstoun.

The other art that attracted him more and more was that of the theatre. From earliest infancy he had more than the usual childish love of dressing up; he several times had parts in David Munir's plays at Cheam; and at Gordonstoun, beginning in the chorus of Gilbert and Sullivan's *Patience*, he continued to keep up his acting. The Queen encouraged this, for she is very conscious of the diffidence that the Prince of Wales has inherited from his grandfather, and remembers the benefit she herself got from the Windsor pantomimes.

It is said in the profession that every great knockabout comedian has a secret ambition to play Hamlet. With the Prince of Wales, it is the converse. Except for that minor role in *Patience*, Gordonstoun had given him no opportunity to play in anything but Shakespeare, although he has always longed to play a comic part, one in which he could make a legitimate fool of himself. His sense of humour, which is strong, is also very simple: the comedy he enjoys most is the Goon type! However, now that he was approaching seventeen and was qualifying for star parts, the Gordonstoun producers did not cast him for Bottom or Dogberry; he had caught their eye in the small part of the Duke of Exeter in *Henry V*, and for the Christmas production of 1965 they asked him to play Macbeth.

He was carrying himself now with much more confidence at school and elsewhere; but to his mother he confessed that he approached this exacting part with great trepidation.

Macbeth, in the judgment of the great Victorian critic Bradley, is 'the most commanding and perhaps the most awe-inspiring figure that Shakespeare drew'; and the Prince of Wales, for whom command lay in the far future, and who had never wished to inspire awe in anybody, felt that it was too much for him. But he began to study the play and the part with his usual conscientious thoroughness, and soon he felt the great mind of Shakespeare imposing its magic upon his. It was not only for the pleasure he has always felt in the music of words and the joy of speaking them, as he does, effectively. He became fascinated with the character of the man he had to portray, perceived the essential nobility within him, and pondered long upon the apparent contradiction between his fine qualities and the dark deeds that bring him to damnation. Such a mixture of good and evil is planted in human nature itself; and as his schooldays drew towards their close the Prince of Wales was coming to feel that the worthiest of all themes of education is the study of the nature of man. In interpreting Shakespeare's tragedy, as however modest an amateur, he was looking into the human heart through the most penetrating eyes that have ever been turned upon it; and he learned to understand the character of Macbeth very much as Dr. Dover Wilson writes of it:

'Not all the blood he spills can extinguish his native humanity or blot out his splendour. Rather, as the play moves to the inevitable catastrophe and we sit watching his soul in process of dissolution, while we never for a moment condone or excuse his crimes, the personality of the man seems to become at once more portentous and more appealing.'

On the night, a fortnight after his seventeenth birthday, his youthful twentieth-century personality disappeared behind a large professionally fabricated wig and beard, and most of his misgivings about his competence with it. The Queen and the Duke of Edinburgh made the journey from London expressedly to attend the performance, and were not disappointed. The mighty verse was delivered in a finely modulated voice; and the tormented character came to life.

He had spent all his schooldays, both at Cheam and Gordonstoun, under the shadow of a more conventionally successful, outgoing, athletic father. Prince Philip had been a star of the playing field, but in the Gordonstoun production of *Macbeth* a generation before he had qualified only for the small part of Malcolm. Here, at any rate, Charles was playing the lead in every sense.

It was not the only success that stood to their son's credit at the end of that Christmas term. He had been made a prefect. He learned that his uphill fight against his most obstinate academic enemy had ended in victory: he had at last satisfied the O-level examiners in mathematics. And one more achievement he knew would specially gratify the father he so much admired.

The Duke of Edinburgh's Award Scheme embodies the same values as those on which Gordonstoun is based—not unnaturally, under the patronage of an Old Boy. Candidates have to submit evidence of their accomplishment in four departments: in rescue work or public service; in endurance on expeditions; in some form of craftsmanship; and in physical fitness. The Prince of Wales had qualified in first aid; by his mountaineering in the Cairngorms; with a series of vessels produced in the pottery workshop; and by his adequate record on the running track. On the last day of term the headmaster was able to put the Duke of Edinburgh's silver medal in his hands.

It had already been made known that the Prince would be leaving Gordonstoun at least temporarily in the New Year: when, if at all, he would return was left uncertain. If in fact this should turn out to be the end of his school career in Scotland, he could go home for Christmas with the knowledge that, after all the laborious and sometimes painful years, there was 'something attempted, something done'.

## { 5 }

# AUSTRALIAN INTERLUDE

BY the time the Prince of Wales reached his seventeenth
birthday he was feeling the need for a break in the
monotony of school life. He was in the mood that makes so
many of his contemporaries appreciate the growing custom
of interposing a free year or six months between the end of
school and any form of higher education. He could not look
forward to any such relief, so the Queen and the Duke of
Edinburgh decided that now was the time to give him a
change. The contrast between their son's naturally introspective temperament and the determinedly outward-look-
ing ideals promulgated by Kurt Hahn for his foundation was
driving him still further in upon himself. It is said that, at
the time when Prince Charles was first entered for Gordonstoun, Dr. Hahn himself had had considerable doubts
whether his school was the most suitable place for this particular pupil. The then Prince Philip of Greece, on the other
hand, had been extremely happy there. When the time
came to choose a school for his son he looked back through
rose-coloured spectacles at his own boyhood and advised
that he could not think of a better choice. The Queen, to
whom, as has already been said, the world of school is a

mystery, readily acquiesced; and the Prince of Wales himself, to whom at thirteen his father was not only the pattern of all the masculine virtues but also his one intimate friend in the elder generation, was enthusiastic to follow in his footsteps. Three years later his devotion was as great as ever; but time had revealed that the natures and talents of father and son were not similar but complementary. For example, to the Duke's considerable disappointment, Prince Charles showed no sign of inheriting his father's technological bent: the one science that attracted him was biology, the study of living things. Nor was he notably drawn towards the sea, although sailing was a particular cult of Gordonstoun: he could perform his duties in a crew efficiently enough, but a sailing craft was a means of getting about by water rather than a joy in itself, like a horse. Those who have sailed with him in the *Bloodhound* say it is the picnic side of the voyage that appeals to him most.

If any of the family inherits the confident extrovert temperament of the Duke of Edinburgh, it is Princess Anne; the Prince of Wales in comparison seems to take after his grandfather, King George VI. His taste in outdoor life runs naturally towards the less gregarious sports. Any older friend of the family visiting him at school would find himself taken for long walks with the Prince among the lonely mountain rocks and burns of Morayshire, while his young host pointed out to him, with deep concentration and apparent expert knowledge, every pool, backwater and eddy where a fish might be expected to rise to the fly. Even in the one passion that father and son conspicuously share, the game of polo, there is a curious distinction between them; to an expert eye, the Prince of Wales already looks like becoming a better horseman than his father, but is never likely to be so good a player.

The Prince spent three years trying with his innate conscientiousness—undoubtedly inherited from King George—to follow in his father's footsteps in all school activities, and in most of them with a creditable measure of success; but he was doing it against the grain. So it was with pleasure and relief that he received his parents' suggestion that he might like a change. Happily his peculiar position made it possible to arrange this without any suggestion of a public snub to Gordonstoun—which would have been monstrously unjust. The masters and boys there had done their very best for the Prince, and if in any sense he had felt himself a square peg in a round hole, that was no fault of theirs. Even if, like his father before him, he had taken the colour of the place without stress or strain, there would still have been strong arguments for giving him at least a taste of some different regimen. He is heir to several Crowns besides that of the United Kingdom; and the earlier he makes acquaintance with the peoples over whom he is destined to reign the better, provided always that it can be managed without disrupting the orderly course of his education. A term or two at some school in the Commonwealth oversea could valuably enlarge his horizons.

The Duke of Edinburgh, as a serving officer in the Navy, had seen something of Australia and been attracted by its people; and since then there had been the memorable Commonwealth Tour. It so happened that Sir Robert Menzies, the most distinguished Australian elder statesman, was visiting Scotland that autumn, and came to stay with the Royal Family at Balmoral. Sir Robert was asked for his advice about schools in Australia, and especially in his own state of Victoria.

Another line of communication was open in the same direction. Since Hanoverian times the clergyman closest to the Royal Family has generally been the Dean of Windsor; a new Dean, Dr. Robin Woods, had been appointed two years before, and had quickly slipped into the accustomed confidential relationship. He had prepared the Prince of

Wales for his confirmation and the Prince had shown a marked liking for his company. Dr. Woods's brother Frank is Archbishop of Melbourne; so that when Sir Robert recommended the Geelong Church of England Grammar School in Victoria the Dean was able to give additional information about it. Other Ministers, at Canberra, Melbourne and Westminster, were drawn into consultation, as was Sir Alexander Downer, the High Commissioner for Australia; and on November 19 it was formally announced in both countries that the Prince of Wales would be entered at Geelong the following term under an arrangement for exchange with an Australian boy, who would take his place at Gordonstoun. (The identity of this boy, to spare him publicity in his own country, was not disclosed until he had left Melbourne secretly on January 16, 1966: he was David Manton, the son of a sheep farmer.) The Prince was to go for one term, in the first instance: not to the school proper, which is comparatively near to Melbourne, but to a kind of colony, about 200 miles to the north, on the lower slope of Mount Timbertop and on the verge of the great gum forests with which it is clothed.

Sir Robert Menzies, who returned home before the announcement was made, was immediately challenged by a Labour member in his own Parliament at Canberra. If the Prince of Wales was coming to Australia, why was he not to attend an ordinary State high school? The former Prince Minister, with his usual good sense, replied, 'I went to Balmoral at the request of the Queen and the Duke of Edinburgh and had a talk with them. I was asked my advice . . . I was quite detached, personally, because I went to another school, which presumably, from the honourable member's question, isn't so exclusive or "tony" . . . I should be very sorry for the young prince if he were at school in the middle of a crowded city in Australia, with people gazing at him, with people trying to get pictures of him, and

with people making him a raree-show. This isn't what he
will be here for. He will be here to go to school and mix
with ordinary Australian boys.'

The Prince of Wales took advantage of his last Christmas
holiday before leaving for the Antipodes to snatch a few
days of winter sports in Liechtenstein with the Prince of
Liechtenstein and his family. The Duke of Edinburgh and
Princess Anne were also in the party.

Prince Philip's three elder sisters and their children have
come to take a high place among the Prince of Wales's
friends. From a personal point of view it is fortunate that
the old princely families have been largely excluded from
the political life of the new Germany since the downfall of
the Hohenzollern Empire in 1918. It thus became possible,
as the animosities of two world wars subsided, for visits to
be exchanged between them and the British Royal Family
without suggestion of any diplomatic overtones. The Queen
had entertained her sisters-in-law and their husbands and
children informally from time to time at Balmoral, Sandringham and Windsor, and without attracting much publicity. She could not return the visits with equal informality,
because of her own position, which makes any appearance
of hers on foreign soil a matter of state. But the Prince of
Wales has become extremely fond of all three of his aunts.
He finds them all completely different; although they share
one characteristic, a mischievous sense of humour. There is
always great excitement at Balmoral when any of them are
coming to stay, and no less when there is a chance to go and
stay with them. The cousins, too, fourteen of them, are
exceedingly popular. Every one of them the Prince of
Wales finds marvellous and funny, and none the worse
company for being very naughty. They seem to him to do
splendid things, he says: and sometimes he envies them the
high spirits of their escapades.

At the end of January the Prince of Wales left London

Airport for Australia. He did not embark on the expedition without interior qualms. Though nine years older, he was still the boy whose childish shrinking from the unknown world of school had lingered in his mother's memory. He was horrified at the thought of going to Australia alone, and thought that the people might take an instant dislike to him. What was he to do if that happened? In these baseless misgivings there is a curious hereditary touch of his grandfather and even his great-grandfather, for both George V and George VI always seemed to confront a new audience with a nervous foreboding of hostility, and were naively surprised when they received unmistakable evidence of the public affection in which they were held.

The Prince of Wales was not, of course, going to Australia literally alone. One of his father's equerries, Squadron Leader David Checketts, whom he had known for several years and liked well, had been detailed to accompany him, and act as a kind of manager of his affairs, maintaining liaison with both the Queen and the Australian governments. (Two governments were involved, that of the State of Victoria at Melbourne and that of the federated Commonwealth at Canberra; both were full of hospitable intentions towards their royal guest, but it was not always easy to harmonize their proposals with one another and with the needs of the Prince's education.) Checketts was not to live at Timbertop, but had taken a lease of a farm some hundred and twenty miles away, where he installed his wife and three small children and set up an office for the conduct of Prince Charles's 'public relations' and a home base for him when not at school. Detective Inspector Derek Sharp, a judo expert, trained in the Metropolitan Police but now serving in Australia, was appointed as body-guard to watch over the Prince of Wales at Timbertop and wherever he might go.

The Qantas aircraft carrying the Prince and his escort

touched down at New York on January 28, 1966. It was the Prince's first visit to the United States, and he saw no more than the airport either here or at the other two stops on his journey, at San Francisco and Hawaii. Flying on over the vast emptiness of the Pacific Ocean, he arrived in Sydney, to be greeted formally by Lord Casey the Governor General and the Prime Minister, Mr. Holt, and went on immediately to the federal capital at Canberra.

That formal reception by the two statesmen at Sydney Airport was the beginning and the end of official pomp in Australia. Almost in the twinkling of an eye the apprehensions Prince Charles had felt about the attitude of the Australian people evaporated into thin air. His fears were dispelled at once by what struck him as their amazing friendliness and good-natured charm. They had no reserve or English shyness and came up to him and said what they liked. He had had one Australian friend in Scotland, but had had no opportunity of talking to him about his country, because the Timbertop project was being kept a secret. So the easy good fellowship of Australia took him completely by surprise. He thought it a very refreshing and active country. Contemplating the bright-eyed pleasure with which he looks back on this experience, one gets a sudden comprehension of the loneliness to which royalty is so easily condemned by the awestruck reverence it commands in England.

The day after arriving in Canberra as a stranger in a strange land Prince Charles was sailing on the lake with Miss Leonie Tyrrell, daughter of Lord Casey's secretary. At home he would probably have been too shy to contemplate anything so adventurous. Like many schoolboys of his parents' generation, but not so many of his own, he had very little experience of the society of girls and was apt to look at them with gingerly caution. Just before leaving England he had come upon his sister dressed up for a party and, the Queen observed with motherly amusement, seemed suddenly to realize for the first time that she too was one of the mysterious siren breed. In the expansive Australian atmosphere the mystery was already losing its terrors, although his acquaintance among the young women of the country was not destined to be very wide.

This placid afternoon on the water was followed by two days of sightseeing round Canberra, including a visit to the wild-life research station at Gungahlin; and on February 3 the Prince of Wales arrived at Timbertop. He had not seen the school proper at Geelong, of which it is an offshoot; when he did, a month later, he had the impression that it was leaning over backwards to be more like an English public school than the original model. Squadron Leader Checketts, with a wider knowledge of English public schools, did not have the same feeling of exaggeration; but the school is undoubtedly copied from the English system. Geelong itself, however, was to play no direct part in the Prince's education. Timbertop, which did, may be considered a variation on another British model, and that a model he knew—Gordonstoun.

Dr. Darling, the former headmaster of Geelong, had been much attracted by the ideas of Kurt Hahn, as applied first at Salem and afterwards at Gordonstoun, and wished to acclimatize them in Australia. But he did not find it possible to fit them to the curriculum of such an orthodox Church of England school as Geelong. He therefore hit on the expedient of setting up a kind of colony in the wilds, to which a whole school generation might emigrate from Geelong for one year of their course—'the spotty year', as he called it, when they were aged fourteen or fifteen. There they could live with the minimum of classroom work, fending for themselves in all possible ways, including the management of such bookwork as they did, and learn something of the self-reliance of the pioneers who opened up the unknown continent of Australia in the days of their ancestors not many generations back. The regime was to be, and is, tougher than that of Gordonstoun; but there on the slope of the Great Dividing Range and on the fringe of the virgin forests still largely uncharted, its primitive quality sprang from the environment, and had none of the artificiality inevitable in comparatively sophisticated Scotland.

There was the usual threat that sophistication would break in, in the form of the insatiable curiosity of the press. It was forty-five years since a Prince of Wales had been seen in Australia—Prince Edward had visited Geelong, but Timbertop did not then exist—and it was too much to expect temptation now to be resisted. So a plan of action had been arranged through the Federal Government before ever the Prince left England. The whole Australian press was invited to send representatives to Timbertop on the day of his arrival. They were left free to follow him everywhere he moved about the grounds, getting to know Timbertop, and permitted to take as many photographs as they liked. But the invitation was coupled with a clear understanding that from thenceforward they should leave the school to continue its daily life undisturbed.

This conditional invitation was accepted in the spirit in which it was offered; and from that moment, Squadron Leader Checketts testifies, the press behaved magnificently. At his farm he received many telephone calls, and he gave out news as and when appropriate. The day after the press party dispersed, the Prince of Wales was out for a cross-country run with the hundred and thirty or so boys in residence, and beginning to settle into an easy relationship with them, which was never disturbed by any outside intrusion.

It would be an exaggeration to say that his acceptance as one of the brotherhood was instantaneous. He was helped by the fact that, in one sense, they were all new boys to-

gether. The others had known one another at Geelong; but
they were just as new to Timbertop as he. Still, he was an
exotic specimen from the other side of the world, quite
apart from being the Queen's son; and he thinks that,
friendly as they were, they were not too sure of him at first.
The questions they asked were searching, sometimes to the
point of embarrassment; and for the first week or ten days
he felt he was on a sticky wicket. Nevertheless, he never felt
self-conscious about his rank, nor did it seem to create any
psychological barrier; what set him slightly apart was the
fact that he was two years older than the general body,
though the effect even of that age-gap was reduced by the
early maturity of Australian boys. There was a simple
explanation of the apparently odd decision to set him down
in the bush among boys so much younger than himself. If he
had gone to the main school at Geelong, he would have
been too unfamiliar with the customs and other boys to
settle in as a prefect, yet would have been unnecessarily
embarrassed if he had not been made one. At Timbertop
his seniority was apparent and he needed no title.

The boys at Timbertop eat together in a communal
dining room; but they live in nine huts, each containing a
'unit' of fourteen or fifteen under a senior described as 'a sort
of N.C.O.'. Charles, as of course he was called by his
schoolfellows here as in Scotland, was appointed one of
these in deference to his age and not to his princely rank. He
did not live with his unit in their hut, but shared a room in
the masters' quarters with another senior boy named Stuart
Macgregor, who had been head of Geelong and had now
come to Timbertop to work quietly for university entry.
Macgregor did a good deal to smooth the new boy's early
path; they were soon on friendly but scarcely intimate
terms.

Although the Prince lived a little apart from his unit, it
was a self-governing community, and the first share in its

government was entrusted to him. His position was different from that which he had occupied as colour bearer at Gordonstoun. There his function had been to maintain liaison between masters and junior boys. Here the unit was in direct confrontation with nature; it must provide for its own welfare without any sort of supervision by masters remote in the background. If mistakes were made it must correct them or suffer the natural effects: there was nobody else to put things right. For example, if the arrangements for heating the water broke down, the unit had to wash in cold until they were working again. It was no use reporting the trouble to authority: there was plenty of timber in the forest and axes to hew logs for stoking the boilers. In any case the Prince remembers there was wood to be chopped nearly every afternoon. Among the trees also there were tasks the unit had undertaken to carry out in aid of the State Forestry Department; the supervision of all such things was not with any master but with Prince Charles, as the unit's appointed chief.

The cult of self-reliance at Timbertop extends into the ordinary teaching, or lack of it. There are few classes; the boys are trusted to do most of their work by themselves. The Prince of Wales did not attend classes at all, since there were none to meet his needs. The Australian boys were preparing for Australian examinations; he, having passed the British G.C.E. examination at various O-levels, was now studying for the A level in French and History. He was determined to pass this test, not to satisfy any external authority but to prove himself to himself. This expedition to Australia, although a valuable contribution to the education of a King, was inevitably a distraction from a schoolboy's course of study. It could be argued that examinations adapted to those who were destined to ordinary professional or industrial life were irrelevant to the needs of one whose future was predetermined; but this was a matter of personal pride. The Prince of Wales was determined to show that, whether or not he was subject to special difficulties, he could surmount the same hurdles as other boys without claiming privilege.

At this stage he really was teaching himself. Academically, as one of his close associates put it, he was thrown in at the deep end. Nearly all his work had to be done by himself. He had brought his books on the two A-level subjects with him, and was left to get on with them independently. He arranged his own time, and was to be subject to no test until he returned to Scotland. Occasionally he read an essay to a tutor or went to visit a supervisor at Geelong, but that was all. He was being introduced, though perhaps he did not quite realize it yet, to the kind of education that Great Britain offers not to the schoolboy but to the undergraduate.

This was deliberate on the part of the headmasters at Geelong and Timbertop, who did not yet know if he would ever again have an opportunity of academic study. This reading for A-levels, like the work being done by the Australian boys for their own national certificate, amounted to the equivalent of the full curriculum of any conventional school. But at Timbertop they had to fit it all in somehow with the immensely strenuous activities which are the real characteristic of the place. Some of these were compulsory, some voluntary; but every boy was expected to take up sufficient voluntary pursuits of his own choice to fill his time. Among the compulsory activities were the cross-country runs across the rugged terrain of mountain and forest. One of them was Prince Charles's first introduction to the Timbertop life; and they came around regularly twice a week. Every weekend was devoted to hiking, in which fifty or sixty miles, carrying camping equipment, might be covered. Once Squadron Leader Checketts came and scrambled with the Prince over successive ridges of the mountains, climbing the equivalent of 11,000 feet and walking 40 miles.

The running and hiking were part of a recurrent routine. The Prince wanted to be in everything that occupied the other boys; but he wanted to do more than they, for the whole country was new to him, and he was determined to see as much of it as was possible in his time, even if it meant, as it sometimes did, neglecting his studies. There were new and fascinating streams to fish, and in this art, with his Scottish experience, he became recognized as the school expert, to whom other boys came for instruction. It was something of a school joke that Charles was always apt to wander off with his rod for hours on end, and leave himself no time for the essay he was supposed to be writing for his tutor.

But there were other activities in which he was a complete novice. He rode out to the sheep stations and helped, with enthusiasm but little skill, in the sheep shearing on which so much of the economy of Australia ultimately depends. He left 'a somewhat shredded sheep'. He hewed down trees. He took part in the Legacy Scheme to help Service Widows. He was inducted into the mysteries of panning for gold, and of gem-hunting at Glenrowan. He went to the Botanical Gardens at Canberra and learned the ornithological technique known as mist-netting.

Some of these mixtures of work and play overflowed into the holidays. Prince Charles had been entered at Timbertop for one term, and the Queen had given directions that the decision whether to stay on for a second should be left entirely to his unfettered choice. He had no hesitation about it. Strangely enough, seeing that the regime of Timbertop is very much that of Gordonstoun carried to a further extreme, he had found his time there as exhilarating as Gordonstoun had lately become irksome. He decided with enthusiasm to stay on, and to devote the autumn holiday to seeing as much of Australia in general as could possibly be crowded in.

The memories of that first term were embodied in a letter which later took shape as an article in *The Gordonstoun Record*, entitled 'Timbertop, or Beating About the Bush'. It deserves substantial quotation, both for its content and as an example of the author's direct unpretentious English.

'Almost everyone', he writes, 'master and boys, enjoy themselves up here'; and it becomes plain that the happiness of Timbertop is of the kind that comes to people whose time is so fully occupied that they never have a moment to consider whether they are happy or not. 'One never seems to stop running here and there for one minute of the day, from 7.30 a.m. breakfast—and no morning run, though there's worse to follow—until the lights go out at 9.15 p.m., having had tea at the unearthly hour of 5.30 p.m. If you have done a cross-country at 4.45 p.m. and arrived back at 5.5 p.m. it's difficult to persuade your stomach to accept food.'

The daily chores are taken cheerfully in his stride: 'Each afternoon after classes, which end at three o'clock, there are jobs which . . . involve chopping and splitting wood, feeding the pigs, cleaning out fly-traps (which are revolting glass bowls seething with flies and very ancient meat), or picking up bits of paper round the School.' This discipline leads on to the greater exertion of the compulsory weekend 'expeditions', designed to prepare the participants for going out for longer periods in the bush, 'where you can't see anything but gum-tree upon gum-tree, which tends to become rather monotonous. . . .

'You virtually have to inspect every inch of the ground you hope to put your tent on in case there are any ants or other ghastly creatures. There is one species of an ant called Bull Ants which are three-quarters of an inch long and they bite like mad! Some boys manage to walk fantastic distances over a week-end of four days or less, and do 130 or even 200 miles.[1] The furthest I've been is 60–70 miles in three days, climbing about 5 peaks on the way. At the campsite the cooking is done on an open fire in a trench. You have to be very careful during hot weather that you don't start a bush fire, and at the beginning of this term [his second] there was a total ban in force, so that you ate all the tinned food cold.'

Such was the simple life of Timbertop in the southern summer from February to May 1966. Before that term ended there was one pleasant episode to remind the Prince of home. Late in March a school week-end exeat allowed him to make a quick trip to Canberra; and there at the airport he met his grandmother Queen Elizabeth, arriving for a tour in Australia. They had a lot of laughs afterwards about it, because it seemed so incongruous to meet each other in the middle of miles of tarmac in Australia. It seemed to them both a good joke that when she got off the plane, and her grandson kissed her, all the crowd started to clap. They drove off to spend two days together in the Snowy Mountains, the Queen Mother as delighted as he was at the encounter, for she has a particularly soft spot for this one of her grandchildren who so closely resembles her late husband in character.

The article in the *Gordonstoun Record* made no mention of the interesting event with which that first term ended, Prince Charles's visit with Mr. T. R. Garnett, the headmaster, and thirty other boys from Geelong and Timbertop to the missionary stations in Papua and New Guinea, the

1. The present writer, who as a subaltern in a half-forgotten war had the honour for a few months of leading a troop of the Australian Light Horse, confesses that those two hundred miles recalled to him his men's hobby of testing the credulity of their young officer with the tallest of tall stories. But if anything of the kind was being tried at the expense of the Prince of Wales, he was quite capable of holding his own at the game:

'I almost convinced one or two Australians outside the School that we rustled kangaroos at Timbertop and that we performed this act by creeping up on them from behind, grabbing them by the tail and flicking them over on to their backs, where you had them at your mercy.'

principal oversea Territory of the Australian Commonwealth. This was an established custom of Geelong, now
being observed for the sixth time; it was generally a holiday
event, but in 1966 was transferred to term time expressly so
that the Prince of Wales might be there.

The journey was made by air, with breaks at Brisbane
and Port Moresby, and a final stage by the Anglican Mission
launch across Goodenough Bay to the principal reception on
the shore by the village of Wedau, near Dogura Cathedral.
Some thousands of people, Australian and Papuan, were
lined up on the beach by the light of the setting sun, some in
formal patches of white or pink, the uniforms of schools,
religious orders and nursing societies, some in the grass
skirts of the island women or the towering feathers of the
men, while the jetty was lined by the church councillors,
splendid with red hibiscus in their hair. An eye-witness
wrote: 'There was no pressing forward for a better view,
but all waited in their places with great dignity and the air
was electric with excitement.' The Bishop, Dr. John
Chisholm, introduced the party and led the Prince of Wales
forward by the hand, to be greeted with a great shout of
'*Egualau!*', which means 'Greeting!' in the Wedauan tongue.
Then, moving informally through the crowd and shaking
many outstretched hands, the Prince clambered on an open
hay trailer which lurched and swayed its way to the Bishop's
house, where he was to lodge.

The following four days were about evenly divided
between religious and secular hospitality. The Prince of
Wales saw every aspect of missionary activity, devotional,
educational, medical and charitable. On the Sunday he was
one of nearly a thousand communicants at the Cathedral
Eucharist, celebrated in the Wedauan language; and at the
parish breakfast which followed, the Bishop wrote, 'it was
very moving to see old men and women coming forward to
speak to him, and one old widow, Phoebe, came forward

with tears of joy in her eyes and in her own language asked
God to bless the Prince and his family'. At other times there
was feasting; there were plays, including a representation of
the landing of the first two missionaries, Albert Maclaren
and Copland King, in 1891; there were presents of objects
of native art for 'Brother Charles' to take back to Buckingham Palace 'to remind him of Wedau'; and on the last night
there was vigorous dancing by the feather-bedecked men
and a more subdued but very graceful exhibition by the
Papuan girls—an entertainment to which the Geelong party
'contributed a somewhat hilarious reel, led by Prince
Charles'.

Several members of the party wrote down their impressions which were subsequently printed at Geelong, and it is
interesting to note which features of four crowded days the
Prince of Wales found most memorable.

'I was given', he wrote, 'some splendid presents including
several mats made from palm fronds—which are always
very useful. I can't help feeling that less and less interest is
being taken by the younger Papuans in the customs and
skills of their parents and grandparents because they feel
that they have to live up to European standards and that
these things belong to the past and have no relevance to the
present or future. This may be a completely false impression, but I was given one or two presents by young people
and when I asked if they had made them, they said their
mothers or aunts had. No doubt, however, in the years to
come, when there are new generations of Papuans, they will
consider these ancient skills of no use. But I expect there will
be those to make souvenirs for tourists; or, if not, I hope a
suitable amount of relics will be preserved for history.'

His young mind was brooding upon the retreat of old and
indigenous cultures before the impact of a sophisticated
civilization. Beyond history, the subject in which he was
preparing to be examined, the Prince of Wales was being

*Above:* With Whisky, September 19, 1959
*Opposite:* Holkham Broad, 1959
*Previous page:* With Flame, 1959
*Overleaf:* Fishing with nets at Loch Muich, August 31, 1959

*Previous page:* Tea in the garden, Balmoral, September 10, 1959
*Above:* Television

*Left:* Hovingham Hall, York: arriving for the reception
following the wedding of the Duke of Kent
*Right:* Ski-ing in Switzerland, January, 1963
*Overleaf:* With Queen Elizabeth

more and more drawn to the science of anthropology, the study of man in all his aspects. At this first contact with a people not yet wholly detached from their primitive roots, still practising the arts they had developed for themselves and not imported, he could not help being saddened by the sight of ancient individual and natural things apparently about to be flattened by the advancing wheels of material progress. When he writes of the dancers he had watched, in their 'magnificent head-dresses of Bird-of-Paradise feathers, cassowary feathers, hornbill beaks and chicken-feathers' one can almost hear him sighing over the prospect of the bowler hats or Beatle haircuts that may so soon supersede this gorgeous plumage.

Yet though this sensitive feeling for living tradition goes deep into Prince Charles's thinking, he is no sentimental mourner over the irrecoverable past; progress on a more spiritual level than that of mere arts and crafts impressed him profoundly in Papua.

'Lastly', his short essay continues, 'I would like to mention how fresh and sincere I found the Church at Dogura. Everyone was so eager to take part in the services, and the singing was almost deafening. One felt that it might almost be the original Church. Where Christianity is new, it must be much easier to enter into the whole spirit of it wholeheartedly, and it is rather wonderful that you can still go somewhere where this strikes you.'

It is impossible to doubt that in these sentences we have direct observation, recorded from the heart. The writer was feeling the excitement of seeing new seed springing up in virgin soil. Squadron Leader Checketts, who was present in Papua, warns us against building too much on the impressions crowded into four days. Nevertheless the Dean of Windsor, who has probably seen deeper into the Prince's inner life than most men, inclines to view the Timbertop months, and especially the brief episode among the Papuans,

as marking the most formative period of his spiritual
development. In Australia he saw a more intelligent Anglicanism than he had yet met with in Britain; and in New
Guinea he had an eye-opener in terms of primitive society,
human nature and religion. Here was the Church of
England really at work in its missions.

The Prince of Wales is bound to be a member of the
established Church of England, of which he will some day
be the Supreme Governor and by whose Primate he will be
crowned. Some young men born to his position might have
revolted against a constitution that seems to deprive a future
king of liberty of conscience. It was never so with Prince
Charles. He has grown up feeling at home in the Church of
England; and he finds in it a breadth of view that allows him to
retain a lively sympathy with the teachings and practice of the
Church of Scotland, which have surrounded him at Balmoral
and Gordonstoun. His confirmation was left by the Queen's
wish to an age when he was sufficiently mature to appreciate its significance fully; and since then he has become a
frequent communicant at Windsor, walking down in the
early morning from the quadrangle to St. George's Chapel
on weekdays as well as Sundays. There is no doubt that he
has developed a genuine religious feeling, and a great sense
of the mystery of life. Those to whom the reticent George
VI spoke on such intimate matters say that in this too the
grandson reminds them strongly of the late King.

The holiday between the two Timbertop terms lasted
only from May 12 to May 31, and the Prince of Wales spent
it in enlarging his knowledge of Australia, chiefly under the
escort of David Checketts. They made a tour down the
East Coast of the continent, staying with private Australians
on the way—except at Sydney, where their host was Roden
(Arthur) Cutler, v.c., the Governor of New South Wales.
On this journey the Timbertop ban on reporters and photographers was not in force, and a good number of them were

generally in pursuit. At Eidsvold in Queensland, for example, a station supporting some seventy thousand head of cattle, the Prince and his hosts spent some time driving twenty of these back and forth through gates and the stockyard, expressly to give a chance to the photographers. He put up such a spectacular show with his small company that he read in the papers next morning, to his great amusement, that he had been driving a herd of four hundred cattle. At the Melanda reserve near Cairns he met Davey Douglas, an aboriginal who was convicted of murder and cannibalism after a tribal fight in the 1920's. Davey assured the Prince that, at seventy, he had given up eating people.

Farther south, in New South Wales, he visited the Peel River Company's estate at Goonoo-Goonoo, and managed to put in a game of polo at a club near by. Polo was by now, as it still is, much his favourite game—perhaps the most conspicuous of the tastes that he shares with his father. The Queen has watched it with a certain ruefulness mingled with her sympathy. It is hard enough for the royal stables to mount one fanatic of the game; two strain their capacity to the utmost. However, the Prince of Wales, since his return from Australia, has been equipped with ponies of his own. Not only has he developed 'an avid passion' for the game: he hopes this passion will never wane. Getting to know his own four ponies, who are all different and so the more exciting, he has high hopes of improving his play (his handicap at present is minus one). Experts who have watched him, however, express doubts whether he will ever be the equal of his father—but for a reason that does him no discredit. He is too considerate, they say, of his mount. The Duke of Edinburgh drives his ponies hard, but his son is always trying to spare them. He will be the better horseman, but will score fewer goals. Still, he was already able at Tamworth to lead his team, and win his match.

From Sydney he went on to the Outward Bound School

on the Hawkesbury River, and then to a carnival given by the Surf Life-Saving Club; but though one of his cherished ambitions had been to try this famous Australian sport, the carnival was not an occasion for beginners, and (Timbertop being deep inland) he never had another opportunity. The short tour ended with a few days on the farm with Squadron Leader and Mrs. Checketts, to whom while he was there another daughter was born—a special delight to the Prince, whose interest in babies remains inexhaustible. To this day both he and Princess Anne prefer to breakfast in the nursery with their little brothers.

The second term at Timbertop was a repetition of the first, modified only by the changing seasons. June and July are the mid-winter months of the southern hemisphere. Snow was coming down in the mountains; and Prince Charles was pressed into service as a ski-instructor. He was alone in his quarters now: Stuart Macgregor, who had shared them at the outset, had left in the middle of the last term, and a successor named John Burnell at the end of it. These were the only Australian boys of his own age with whom he had been brought into close contact; and with neither of them had he established any real intimacy.

His naturally introspective character seems to engender barriers which he himself recognizes and would like to remove, but which still baffle him as they have done since early days at Cheam. He continues to feel that others who should be his intimates are restrained by the fear that any spontaneous advances they might make would be set down as toadying. It is still with those who are too old or too young to be suspected of such motives that he feels most comfortable. All who see him in their company agree that he has a wonderful way with children. He gets on excellently with older people, paying graceful deference to seniority but speaking his own mind frankly. But with his own contemporaries, outside his near kindred, he has yet to achieve any deep relationship. He suffers perhaps more than he knows from one of the inevitable inhibitions of royalty. 'Poor child!' said King George VI in South Africa, watching Princess Elizabeth go out alone to perform some formal function—'she'll always be so lonely.' It was not long before the Princess escaped from that loneliness by way of marriage and a broadening family life; but for her son at seventeen it was accentuated by his innate sensitiveness. He knows that in the sort of life that lies ahead of him a thick skin is an almost necessary defence; but he realizes that he does not possess it, and that it may take a long time to develop. Meanwhile, he knows, he must just grin and bear it.

So in that second term at Timbertop he was externally and very happily absorbed in all the varied activities of a vigorous and friendly crowd, all younger than himself; yet at the same time he was mentally somewhat isolated. Isolation of this kind, however, had its advantages. He was now reading hard for his A-level examination a year ahead; and every moment not occupied in the forest and the fields had to be devoted to his books. Of the two subjects he was to offer, French, thanks to early discipline at home, could largely be taken in his stride. So most of his reading was in history; and before the end of term in July he felt sufficiently confident of his progress to stand up before his schoolfellows and give them a lecture on Charles I. The choice of subject throws its own sidelight on the mind of the lecturer at this time. What he had to say did not derive entirely from the set books he had been reading. 'The saddest of all kings' was personally alive to his imagination as to few boys of his age. His thoughts may have originally turned that way because Charles I was his namesake. But more than that, Charles Stuart stood to him for the tragic romance of ancient things. Windsor is full of memories of King Charles. His body lies in St. George's Chapel. The paintings he procured, including the noble portraits of himself and his family by Sir Anthony

Van Dyck, are still the nucleus of the famous collection that adorns the walls of the state apartments. In the Dean's study, which became so familiar to this later Charles when he was being prepared for confirmation, is the table on which the body of their slain master was laid out for burial by the faithful band of defeated men who had brought it through the snow from the scaffold in Whitehall. Prince Charles had gazed upon this sombre relic with an ever-increasing fascination. The king had come to be for him the key figure in the immemorial history of England, the sense of whose continuity through the ages was perhaps the deepest feeling that his education had fostered in his heart.

That continuity of life in the old country, he realized, was part of the inheritance of the new countries of the Commonwealth; and in this communication of his feeling he was speaking his last words to Australia. Or nearly his last. For a final message on the day of his departure he wrote a few sentences in manuscript, which his equerry read aloud to the reporters and others gathered at the airport:

'It would be difficult to leave without saying how much I have enjoyed and appreciated my stay in Australia and how touched I have been by the kindness of so many people in making these six months such a worthwhile experience. The most wonderful part was the opportunity to travel and see, at least, some of the country (I hope I shall be able to come back and see the rest) and also the chance to meet so many people which completes the link with a country I am very sad to be leaving; and yet I shall now be able to visualize Australia in the most vivid terms, after such a marvellous visit.'

## { 6 }

# THE END OF SCHOOL

THE winter term at Timbertop ended in July, and the
Prince of Wales, with Squadron Leader Checketts in
attendance, took flight for home. In the half-year of his stay
in Australia the crowding succession of new experiences had
changed him perhaps more than he knew. Certainly the
masters at Timbertop were very conscious of his rapid
development in self-confidence. They remembered him on
his first arrival as a tousle-headed schoolboy with an
'English' complexion, who had evidently been well brought
up. He had been shy and self-conscious, very pleasant and
polite but a little on edge. When he left he was relaxed, sure
of himself as a person and—a high compliment on Australian lips—unaffected by the fact that he was Prince of Wales.
He was returning to England, however, well aware of the
part for which he was cast and which he must soon begin to
play in earnest; and no less aware were the people among
whom he and Checketts paused on the stages of their homeward journey. They went by way of Auckland, to give the
Prince a brief glimpse of New Zealand, and then on across
the Pacific Ocean, touching down only at Tahiti. They
made a longer stop in Mexico City, where the Prince stayed

with the British Ambassador, Sir Nicolas Cheetham, and had time to visit the mysterious pyramids of Teotihuacan. These monuments of a vanished civilization, some dating from the sixth century, were probably the oldest buildings he had yet seen, and provided more food for his constant hunger for understanding of the past. The Ambassador gave a private party to which were invited a number of the most beautiful ornaments of Mexican society. The Prince of Wales greeted them with impeccable politeness; but, so far as Squadron Leader Checketts could see, none of them aroused the slightest interest in him. There was a marked contrast a few months later, when the Queen gave a young people's dance at Windsor for her eldest son and her daughter. Although he dances well and enjoys it, he had seemed frightened of girls at a similar function the previous Christmas, just before he went to Australia. But now the Queen sat out with a friend, laughing quietly with him as they observed the enthusiasm with which the Prince of Wales sought out all the prettiest partners in the room to dance with. Only a Gordonstoun term had intervened since his heart had refused to flutter in Mexico: he could scarcely have undergone an internal revolution. The inference seems to be that he has now his established preferences in female loveliness, and that his taste runs rather to the rosebuds of England than to the tiger lilies of the tropic south.

While he had been away at Timbertop deep thought had been given to the next stages in his future. This had been the purpose of a dinner party which the Queen gave at Buckingham Palace on December 22, 1965. The guests were the Archbishop of Canterbury, the Prime Minister, Lord Mountbatten as representative of the heads of all the defence services, Sir Charles Wilson of Glasgow, who was then the Chairman of the Committee of Vice-Chancellors, and the Dean of Windsor. After dinner the Queen invited them to form themselves there and then into a committee, under the chairmanship of the Duke of Edinburgh, and advise her on how the education of her son should continue after he left school. She herself remained and listened to their discussion, but did not intervene. Her Principal Private Secretary, Sir Michael Adeane, who was at the dinner table, was asked to act as secretary to the committee.

The discussion ranged widely, for the participants approached the subject from very different points of view, although in their own education they had a good deal in common. The Archbishop and the Dean were from Cambridge, the Prime Minister and the Vice-Chancellor from Oxford; even the Admiral, who was a product of the Naval Colleges at Osborne and Dartmouth, had as a junior officer been seconded for a short course of study at Christ's College, Cambridge. The committee had in effect to forge —or advise the Queen how to forge—one more link in the long chain of developing tradition which is outlined in the appendix on the upbringing of the heirs to the Throne. Centuries of custom prescribed that a Prince of Wales should not only wear the uniforms of the services, but gain practical experience in the junior commissioned ranks of at least one. The innovations of more recent reigns were creating a new custom of university education. Edward VII had spent short periods at three universities, though never permitted to immerse himself in undergraduate life. Edward VIII had had something much more like a normal course at Oxford. Albert, Duke of York, had gone from the Navy to Cambridge, at a time when it could not be foreseen that he would one day be King George VI. There were, it would seem, two equally respectable conventions to be reconciled —and brought up to date.

A great many points of detail were considered, without reaching agreement, and left for settlement at a later meeting. But the five members of the committee, as the hour grew late, found that they could at least concur in some broad general recommendations to the Queen. First, the Prince of Wales ought to go to a university. He might even go to more than one, and in that event universities in the Commonwealth oversea should not be excluded from consideration. Secondly, whatever service training might be thought necessary, the university course should have precedence in time. Thirdly, and as a logical corollary, when the time came for considering the services, the Queen was reminded of the comparatively new approach to a commission by way of university entry rather than training at Dartmouth, Sandhurst or Cranwell.

The Prince of Wales had not been present at the dinner, but of course was informed at once of the committee's recommendations. He was of an age now to have the principal voice in deciding his own future; he had had more than enough of school and was eager to get away. The proposal that he should go soon to the university was entirely in accord with his inclinations, as well as those of his parents. The only substantial doubt was which university should be chosen; and he went off to Timbertop with this not finally decided. The four ancient Scottish universities might be considered; but by the time he left he would have been nearly five years at Gordonstoun, and it was clear that Scotland had had at least its fair share in his education. Though Balmoral is his favourite home among the four royal residences, he does not feel the Scottish element in his blood, coming from his grandmother, is in any way dominant. So he looked to the English universities; and here his range of choice was quickly narrowed. The time may come when a Prince of the Royal House may enter his name at one of the so-called 'Redbrick' foundations; but for Prince Charles they lack the indispensable appeal. He was, and is, at an age when many boys tend either to fall in love with tradition or to rebel violently against it. He was among the lovers: tradition seemed to him the foundation of all our lives, though if you think the word has acquired overtones that some modern people distrust, he will let you call it habit. Now especially, when he was inclined to react psychologically against a protracted spell at an untraditional school, the first requisite for the next stage of his education was a sense of contact with the living past. Moreover, the deep love he had developed for ancient architecture urged him in the same direction. In short, the essential choice was between Oxford and Cambridge. He had his time at Timbertop, perhaps a little more, in which to make up his mind. He was aided, of course, by letters from home; and when he returned he had made his decision: he would go to Cambridge. He would be following in the footsteps of his grandfather, King George; and his exceptionally strong family feeling made that an important consideration. Cambridge is not very far from Sandringham, and he knew the city fairly well. It was the university of his favourite British cousins, Prince William and Prince Richard of Gloucester, whom he had visited at Magdalene, and who had given him an attractive picture of their undergraduate life. But what drew him most compellingly was the architectural glory of the place, and especially of King's College Chapel, the beauty of which moves him deeply, a masterpiece of the same English perpendicular style as his familiar St. George's, Windsor.

But the Prince of Wales has not gone to King's. The choice of a College was still open when he went back to Gordonstoun for the Christmas term; and the Queen asked the Dean of Windsor to visit Cambridge on her behalf and advise her and her son which to select. Dr. Woods called on the Vice-Chancellor and a number of Heads of Colleges and put searching questions to them all. He picked on five colleges as possible, made further inquiries into these and submitted a detailed and impartial report to the Queen, balancing their various merits and defects. It came back to

him with a message that he must make a definite recom-
mendation. This he did. He set aside one college as rather
colourless; another as setting itself up wilfully to be socially
exclusive; a third, though a great foundation with a splendid
history, because it happened to be going through a phase of
chaotic personal relations between the dons.

He delivered final judgment in favour of Trinity. It was
King George VI's college, and a royal foundation. The
Dean gave several reasons for his choice. A Trinity fellowship has always been regarded in the outside world as the
blue riband of Cambridge learning, and the dons are today,
the Dean reported, of outstanding calibre. At the head of
them the Master, Lord Butler, though a somewhat enigmatic personality, has been known for many years to the
Royal Family as a statesman of the highest rank in the service
of the Queen and her father before her. But the factor that
chiefly influenced the Dean was the comprehensive character
of the undergraduate body of the college—considerably the
largest in the university. Three-quarters of the whole had
come up from grammar schools; here the Prince of Wales
would have the chance to mix with and make friends among
all ranks and classes of his future subjects. Nothing could be
more essential to the development of a twenty-first-century
King.

Neither the Queen nor the Duke of Edinburgh has any
inside knowledge of universities; and Prince Charles's own
ideas were probably vaguer than those of many English
schoolboys of eighteen, for Gordonstoun is rather remote
from the academic world even of Scotland. All three therefore were very willing to be guided by the Dean's carefully
considered advice. Though he was in fact recommending his
own College, they knew Dr. Woods well, and had no
doubt that he was incapable of intruding a personal bias. To
Trinity College the Prince of Wales, with the cordial assent
of Master and Fellows, decided to go.

Meanwhile the September term had opened at Gordonstoun. The Prince of Wales, on his return, found himself
installed as 'Helper' for Windmill Lodge; and the following
term he succeeded to the position of Guardian. It was a
greater promotion than he had expected when he came home
from Australia; and as recently as the beginning of August
1966 the Queen had still been speculating on his chances of
even becoming captain of his house, Windmill Lodge. The
Guardian is the head boy of the whole school. He is not perhaps quite so imposing a dignitary as the President of Pop
at Eton or Praefect of Hall at Winchester. He has not the
power of the rod, which is reserved to housemasters, and
seldom exercised by them; nor is there any fagging system.
His position is one of influence rather than defined authority,
and within limits may be very much what the individual
holder chooses to make of it. As the Prince of Wales interpreted it, the most important function of the Guardian was
to maintain liaison between the headmaster, the housemasters and the boys, the senior boys especially. He was the
mouthpiece of public opinion; he could, if need arose, act as
a kind of Ombudsman. His prescribed functions amounted
to little more than making out lists from time to time
and seeing that boys generally performed their school duties
—a light responsibility in a school where so much is entrusted to the individual's sense of honour. But if suggestions
or petitions came up from the rank and file, it was for the
Guardian to formulate them and bring them to the notice of
the headmaster or housemasters. A good Guardian is in
pretty frequent touch with these; and one test of his success
is the degree to which the lines of communication between
masters and boys are kept open. In this respect the Prince of
Wales perhaps reflected on the analogy between his duties
and that of his mother's private secretaries, one of whose
main tasks is to see that the Sovereign is kept informed of
all movements of opinion among her subjects that she

should know of, and that her own personality and thoughts are accurately presented to the world.

The Prince of Wales's acknowledged success in this by no means easy position was evidence that he had developed considerably from the rather diffident boy who had left for Australia less than a year before. He now felt much more confident in his power to master circumstance, and even his inherited shyness bothered him less. He does not think his new self-confidence derived much, if anything, from his status as Guardian; there is no tradition at Gordonstoun of venerating the office as such: the Guardian has to win respect by his own character. He has to work for this respect, and it takes quite a long time to establish his position—or so the Prince thinks from his own experience. The tempo of his life was changing; a new purposefulness was apparent. When he telephoned Miss Anderson on his return from Australia, she asked him how he felt. 'Oh—no time to feel anything—too busy!' he replied.

There can be little doubt that the increased sureness of touch in human relations, the firmer and therefore happier self-reliance, was the contribution that Australia had made to the future King's equipment for life. He is too modest to speak of his achievements as Guardian; but he sometimes had delicate situations to handle. There was, for example, an unhappy occasion when the Headmaster decided that two boys must be expelled. The Guardian fully recognized the gravity of their offence. But he was very much distressed by this way of dealing with it. In his view it was an abdication of responsibility: the proper course was to keep them at school and try to make them better—not turn them out, perhaps to go to the bad in a less-disciplined environment. His argument did not prevail—no doubt authority was more conscious than he of its responsibility to the rest of the school community—but his stand for what he believed in commanded respect.

A significant date in the Prince's life occurred in the middle of his last autumn term—his eighteenth birthday. There is a hardy illusion that crops up year after year to the effect that at eighteen a member of the Royal Family comes of age. The legend has no foundation. At Common Law the Sovereign is always of age; no other person comes of age before twenty-one—unless we accept the ingenious theory of the late Mr. Iwi (see p. 20 above) which would have brought Prince Charles to legal maturity at the age of three. But by the statute law of the present century the Heir Apparent acquires certain privileges not enjoyed by other minors. Should he accede to the Throne at eighteen or over he can exercise the full powers of the Crown without a Regent; in case of the Queen's total disablement, he himself becomes the Regent. A much less hypothetical privilege is that, once he is eighteen, he takes his place as first of the four adults nearest to the succession who act for the Queen as Counsellors of State when she is absent from the country. (The other three, one of whom in due course will be Princess Anne, must be at least twenty-one.) Queen Elizabeth and the Duke of Edinburgh, if not abroad with the Queen, are also Counsellors.

These are the only exceptional personal rights which come to the Heir Apparent at eighteen. There is also one financial privilege which belongs to him only indirectly. The estates of the Duchy of Cornwall, which provide an income for the Heir Apparent without any grant from the taxpayer, bring in a revenue of at least £90,000 a year. By an arrangement made at the Queen's accession, £10,000 of this was to come to her during her son's childhood; the remainder was handed over to the Treasury to set against the Civil List— the annual income voted to her by Parliament in return for her customary surrender of the much larger rent-rolls from the Crown Lands. When the Prince reached the age of eighteen the £10,000 was increased to £30,000; but it is still paid to the Queen on his behalf, and not to him. When he comes of age in 1969 he will be entitled to full control and enjoyment of the whole revenue of the Duchy, which is believed to, with the fall in the value of money, amount to more than three times the £90,000 at which it was estimated some years ago.

Although his eighteenth birthday was a technical milestone on the road to manhood, the only change it was at all likely to introduce into the Prince's life was a possible summons from time to time to take his place as a Counsellor of State. This first occurred in July 1967, when the Queen attended the Canadian centenary celebrations at Montreal; but it was not found necessary to interrupt the Prince's last term at school. Any two of the Counsellors can act for them all; and there have been many occasions when Queen Elizabeth and Princess Margaret, especially in the old days when they were living together at Clarence House, performed all the formal duties, signing papers or even holding Privy Councils, on behalf of the absent Queen. Something of the same kind could have been done again, had any issue requiring formal legal action arisen during the few days of the Queen's Canadian visit.

A more exciting prospect on his eighteenth birthday was that at last he was to fulfil one of his most cherished ambitions. Ever since he had begun to enjoy acting he had longed to play a comic part. But apart from an appearance in the chorus of *Patience* the Gordonstoun stage had never seen him except in Shakespeare. The exhilaration of speaking the great poetry to the best of his powers had given him great pleasure; but still there was that hankering to raise a laugh. Now at last the school was to perform *The Pirates of Penzance*; and the Guardian was delighted to be cast for the Pirate King. It gave him the chance to exercise his well modulated singing voice; but what he really valued was the prospect of making a legitimate fool of himself. He enjoyed the rehearsals; he found the performance on the night glorious fun. With the laughter and the applause, led by his mother and father who had come north to support him, which greeted his final curtain, he could feel that the last of his school ambitions had been triumphantly achieved.

Or the last but one. There still loomed ahead the final test of the A-level examination in History and French. He had come back to Gordonstoun after Timbertop mainly because he wished to go through with this task. Although Trinity would certainly not insist on this qualification, he was determined to show that he could do what was required of other freshmen without having to rely on privilege. He sat for the examination in July 1967; and early in September his success in both subjects was announced[1].

But school successes of all kinds were beginning to dwindle in his maturing eyes as he surveyed the little world in which he had been living. In one sense, with the fight over his old obsessive diffidence largely won, he was more at home there than before he went away to Australia; and he realized that he would not leave without a certain sadness. But having seen wider horizons, he was very much aware that he could not confine himself within these limits much longer without danger of atrophy. He still from time to time feels a sudden pang of longing to go back to Australia, to the freshness and exhilaration of Timbertop. It is a per-

1. Mr. R. M. Todd, secretary of the Oxford and Cambridge Schools Examination Board, reported in *The Times* of October 5, 1967, says the Prince 'shone' in his optional history paper—'the one which marks out the "high flyers" as regards judgment, initiative, and historical acumen. If a boy has done well in this paper—and the Prince got a distinction—it is a very good guide to university.'

Mr. Todd says only just over six per cent of the board's 4,000 or so history candidates won distinctions in the special paper. 'I consider that his performance was extraordinary, especially when you consider that he was digging about in Australia and that kind of thing beforehand. He has so many things to do, he must have worked like a demon. I should hesitate to tackle the paper myself, it takes me back to the time when I did Greats.'

fectly natural attitude; these last terms at Gordonstoun were a mere pendant to his schooldays. In the inner life of the imagination, which to him had always been the deeper reality, he was already an undergraduate, eager to explore the widening vistas which would soon be opening ahead. In this new perspective the whole activity of school was coming to look rather petty, even pathetic. Sometimes he could not help laughing at it all; and then he would check himself, because to mock at what a year or two ago had seemed so important would be unfair to Gordonstoun; and as the time of parting drew near his always tender conscience was telling him how grateful he should be for all that this place, unsympathetic as it seemed at some times, and tedious at others, had done to nourish his character.

Coming as he does from a family background without university associations, and from a school standing a little apart from English or Scottish educational orthodoxy, the Prince of Wales went up to Trinity in October 1967 with only a vague impression of what he would find there.[1] Partly for that reason, it is probable that he will gain from Cambridge more than their time at the university gave to any of the short list of previous Sovereigns—Edward VII, Edward VIII and George VI—who have experienced it in modern times. This is not solely because he intends to live the normal unprivileged undergraduate life—in college rooms on the first floor, where he will not be plagued by sightseers at the window. The deeper reason is that he is at heart an academic, though until now the academic side of his education has been restricted. An older friend, both intimate and shrewd, who has already been quoted here more than once, feels sure that, born and trained in different circumstances, he would have made a first-class schoolmaster, teaching in the humanities. This is a judgment of his tem-

1. It was necessary for this book to be in the hands of the printers before the beginning of the Prince's first term at Cambridge.

perament, not of his present scholastic equipment. He is not learned; but he has an open and inquiring mind, a capacity and desire to learn. He is more clearly designed to be a student than any Sovereign since James I, though unlike the 'British Solomon' he has nothing of the pedant in him. And if his thirst for knowledge is more probably derived from a nearer ancestor, his robustly simple sense of humour will save him from ever taking himself quite so seriously as Albert the Prince Consort.

His tutor at Trinity, the Fellow of the College appointed to give him guidance and counsel in his personal life, is Dr. D. M. Marrian, who is an organic chemist. But although the Duke of Edinburgh would like his son to acquire some scientific knowledge, the only science in which he has expressed any interest is biology, which he does not regard as anything but a sideline. At school he was given no instruction specially designed for his needs as Heir to the Throne—such as his mother, who was not going to a university, received from Sir Henry Marten, the Provost of Eton. At Cambridge the intention is that he shall be given some teaching in constitutional law, a subject to which he should be readily attracted by his bent for history.

But his principal interest is in exploring the penumbra of history, the life of peoples who have no written record, either because they have not attained to a literate civilization, or because they lived in ages before literacy was achieved. Prehistory, archaeology, anthropology are aspects of this study. Prince Charles's interest had been stimulated as much by the barbaric rituals of the Papuan islanders as by the enigmatic remains of possible prehistoric cavemen that he unearthed beneath the cliffs of Elgin. And for these reasons he has chosen to study archaeology and physical and social anthropology during his first year. He also feels that he ought to know something of economics, even if it requires some return to mathematics in order to understand it.

When he first decided to go up to Cambridge, Prince Charles was averse from the idea of reading for the Tripos; he hoped to do a special course, in which his outside interests —extending even so far as the elements of medicine—might be included. In the next few months, however, his ideas changed a little, and friends whose judgment he respects have suggested that, although he has no reason to seek a degree for its own sake, the prospect of an examination at the end of his course would give system and direction to his reading. The Master of Trinity is clearly of this opinion; he is hoping that Prince Charles will spend his full three years at Cambridge and will sit for the two Tripos examinations which would qualify him to become a Bachelor of Arts at once and a Master of Arts without further examination four years later; and his former schoolmasters and other qualified judges are confident of his ability to obtain an honours degree.

Whether he reads for the Tripos or not, Prince Charles is keen to extend his archaeological studies into practical work. He hopes to go and dig somewhere interesting in vacations; and the Dean of Windsor cherishes a plan to take him in the long vacation on a tour among the relics of ancient civilizations in Italy, Greece and Palestine.

Cambridge has two long-established acting societies—the Footlights and the Amateur Dramatic Club—besides a habit of collecting companies on a college basis for the perform- ance of particular plays. There will be plenty of opportunity for Prince Charles to continue his theatrical career in these. There is also a distinguished tradition in the university for the production of the masterpieces of the Attic theatre: but although Prince Charles has a smattering of Greek, picked up rather unexpectedly at Timbertop, he does not think his classical scholarship is quite a match for the profundities of Aeschylus or the wit of Aristophanes.

Rather curiously, considering that he began acting himself

while still at Cheam, his interest in the professional stage developed later. But, particularly after seeing a performance of Sheridan's *The Rivals* at Christmas, 1966, he has suddenly found that he loves the theatre. He went to plays as often as he could in the following Easter holidays, his last from Gordonstoun; Cowes and Balmoral, of course, in the summer months after leaving school, are not theatrical centres, but he may well become a familiar figure in the stalls in coming university vacations. He generally goes, like his mother and aunt at the same age, in parties of six or eight young people. It is unfortunate that, if he happens to be seen sitting next to an eligible girl in the car going or coming, the tongues and pens of the gossip-writers are immediately set wagging; but he has grown to recognize this as one of the occupational hazards which he has to grin and bear, hoping that he will develop a thicker skin by and by.

In music as in drama he considers his taste is only just being formed—although he has played a variety of instruments for half his nineteen years: first the piano, then the trumpet and now the 'cello. He has played in a piano concerto by Schumann and delights in playing Bach and Mozart —particularly the Mozart Piano Concerto No. 4, which he describes as the most wonderful musical experience he has yet had. He prefers the eighteenth-century composers to their nineteenth-century successors and finds a great deal of modern music merely discordant, although he acknowledges that some of it, well played and well sung, has grown on him after the third or fourth hearing. Certainly he enjoyed singing in Benjamin Britten's *St. Nicholas*, but only after several rehearsals.

Pop music he leaves for Princess Anne, and sees in it one of the more striking examples of the divergence in tastes that has sprung up between himself and his sister since they both went to school. They are as fond of one another as ever, but they are 'not like in like but like in difference'.

Their circles of friends are quite distinct, seldom over-lapping. But this does not prevent them from spending a lot of time happily in each other's company during the holidays: Princess Anne does not yet go out very often to parties, and Prince Charles by his own choice goes even less frequently. Up to the time of leaving Gordonstoun he felt that he was so much away at school that it was generally more fun to stay at home when he had the chance. His sister gambols cheerfully around, meeting people and enjoying it, with the expansive good-fellowship of her father. The Prince of Wales, like his mother, does not take easily to the duty of constantly smiling at people he does not know. But there is no doubt that the character that is reborn in him is that of his grandfather, King George VI. They had different up-bringings, and different tastes and talents. But the key to Prince Charles's idiosyncrasy is King George's great sensi-tivity to other people's thoughts and feelings: what they feel about themselves, what they think about him. He has the same great care for other people—as was shown in his reaction to the expulsion of those two boys from Gordons-toun.

He was rather late in acquiring a taste for reading—the Queen, like many less exalted parents, blames television for this—but he reads a good deal for pleasure now. He is con-scious of gaps in his knowledge of literature: although he loves reading Shakespeare as well as acting him, there are many other great writers with whom he is not yet acquainted. He expects to widen his range greatly at Cambridge.

For lighter reading he prefers books of mystery, adventure and humour, and the classics of his parents' and grand-parents' generation rather than his own: Sherlock Holmes, John Buchan, P. G. Wodehouse. But in the last year or so he has devoted more and more time to historical biographies—he read several while he was in Australia. In his last holidays from Gordonstoun he finished Randolph Churchill's volume on his father's youth, which he found fascinating, and started on Sir Winston's own account, *My Early Life*. He enjoyed the memoirs of Margot Asquith and thought Lytton Strachey's *Queen Victoria* a marvellous book. He was much impressed by Robert Ardrey's *African Genesis*, which clearly attracted him because of his interest in prehistory, anthropology and the study of evolution.

He has not kept up his painting, despite the early promise that he showed, mainly because there are too many other demands on his time. But after living so long among the masterpieces that cover the walls at Windsor, and in boyhood scarcely giving them a thought, he has recently begun to take notice of them and appreciate the magnificent collection that surrounds him. The artists of the Dutch and Flemish schools appeal most to him. He loves Rembrandt and Van Dyck, and gets a great deal of enjoyment from Rubens, despite 'all that pink flesh' that some people find a little overwhelming. This admiration for the painters of the seventeenth century is very much in keeping with his special feeling for Charles I—not so much as the crusader for a concept of kingship that history has repudiated, but as the sensitive lover of beauty who patronized and was portrayed by some of these masters and who laid the foundations of the Royal collections. He does his best to appreciate the moderns; but though he admires, for instance, the exquisite draftsmanship of the early Picasso he finds his later works 'rather gruesome'.

All these interests, and many others, will have scope for growth at Cambridge, but most significant of all, and most incalculable, will be the plunge into the whirlpool of undergraduate social life. Prince Charles is looking forward to this with an exhilarating sense of liberation. He cannot be relieved of the inevitable detective (and himself foresees possible situations in which he might be grateful for his presence), but the detective will be lodged in another part of the college and is expert at making himself as inconspicuous as possible. Apart from that—and unlike previous heirs to the Throne—he takes no personal retinue to the university. Squadron Leader Checketts, now accredited directly to him as equerry and no longer borrowed from his father, has opened an office for him in Buckingham Palace, and will remain there to manage his official relations at long range. This service may well resolve itself largely into a matter of keeping politely at bay large numbers of well-wishing and loyal people who are anxious to involve the Prince of Wales in this, that or the other ceremonial or deserving public activity. It is still the Queen's desire that no avoidable engagement shall be allowed to disturb his education.

So he has greater opportunities than any prince before him to take a full part in university life, to join what undergraduate clubs he pleases, to play any game that appeals to him (including polo, at which it will not be surprising to see him soon scoring goals against Oxford), to dine in hall, to attend college concerts, to entertain and to be entertained, to make friends of his own seeking. Here if anywhere he should find an answer to the misgivings sometimes expressed by those who observe his ease of intercourse with young children or with people much older than himself, but do not see him taking many contemporaries into his intimacy. In the great variety of young people, of all social backgrounds, whom he will meet at Trinity or in the university at large, he cannot fail to find kindred spirits.

He will, it is to be hoped, eat, drink and be merry with them; and he will argue as undergraduates have done from time immemorial. It might be thought that in this he would feel inhibited, for there has never been a more politically minded undergraduate generation than today, and he might feel cramped by the convention that one so near to the Throne must not publicly take sides in party politics. He does not, however, think that this will cause him serious trouble. He never shrank from expressing controversial opinions at Gordonstoun, and he thinks he knows by this time how to keep his bolder thoughts within the bounds of private occasions and hold his peace when there is any danger of their being given publicity.

In the course of undergraduate discussion, as in his formal studies, the Prince of Wales is exposed to a much greater variety of conflicting opinions than he ever heard expressed at school, or even in palaces. He is fully prepared to find many beliefs challenged that he has hitherto taken for granted, and to change some of them as his experience widens. He is conscious of being at an age at which thinking may be particularly fluid. For instance, that lecture which he gave at Timbertop on Charles I already seems to him immature. His interest in the subject is unabated, and he has continued his reading about the King who is to one party 'the Royal Martyr' and to their adversaries 'the Man of Blood'; and he realizes that no more at nineteen than at seventeen can he reach a final judgment in a controversy that has divided the learned for more than three centuries. This is only an example of a general process of self-criticism that will be fundamental to his education at the university. Many a freshman before him has gone up with strong convictions and been surprised to find them repudiated by his contemporaries; has reacted to an equally uncompromising position in the opposite sense; and has then spent the rest of his time at the university, sometimes the rest of his life, finding the middle ground on which he can rest. The Prince of Wales, as has been said, was drawn to Cambridge largely by his love of tradition—which to some people represents the wisdom of the ages, and to others is the distillation of what Gibbon called 'the register of the crimes, follies and misfortunes of mankind'. Whether his youthful romanticism will survive the stresses of academic debate we do not know—and he does not know; and the same is true of all other opinions he at present holds. According to one school of philosophy the pursuit of truth leads from thesis to antithesis and eventually to synthesis; and from this universal process the minds of princes are not exempt.

Though the Queen's wise determination to shield her son from publicity until his education is complete is unabated, there are some occasions when the strong magnetism of the Constitution, drawing him towards the limelight, cannot reasonably be withstood. Once he had officiated according to law, in however passive and theoretical a manner, as a Counsellor of State, it would have been illogical to withhold his presence from the greatest of the annual ceremonies of royalty. According to a doctrine going back at least as far as Sir John Fortescue, Chief Justice under Henry VI, the moment of supreme majesty for the Sovereign is when he presides over the Lords and Commons of the land assembled for the state opening of Parliament. It was clearly time for the Prince of Wales to take part in this splendid gathering; and accordingly the Queen directed that, at the opening of the new session in November 1967, he should drive in state from Buckingham Palace, and take his seat in the traditional place of the Heir, in a chair of state on the right of the Throne.

A still more significant introduction to public life awaits him in 1969, when the Queen has announced that she will fulfil her long-standing promise to present her son to the Welsh people at Caernarvon. He will spend the summer term at the University College of Aberystwyth, to acquire some knowledge of Wales and its language; and the ceremony will be performed in the roofless castle on the first of July. It will presumably be preceded by the accolade of knighthood and investiture at the June Chapter of the Order of the Garter at Windsor. Calls for further public appearances are sure to follow. In any case he comes of age on November 14, 1969, which will be at the beginning of his final year for the Tripos, assuming that he decides to read for a degree.

To look beyond that is pure speculation. One of the few who know the Prince of Wales intimately enough to speculate responsibly, asks 'What on earth are we to do with him for the next forty years?' 'We' in this context no doubt means, not the speaker and his friends, but the nation at large, which shapes the lives of princes who are to represent it. The question will not arise for several years, and by then the Prince himself may be trusted to answer it. He has an open mind; he is intellectually rather young for his years; his whole manner of thinking may be profoundly changed by the experiences that await him at the university. From there, in all probability, he will go on to one or more of the services, where the training will keep him something more than busy for not less than two years. The problem of his occupation can scarcely become urgent till at least four years hence. By that time there may well be, actually or in prospect, a Princess of Wales, whose unknown personality will also have to be taken into account.

The point that needs emphasis is that the heir is not just an actor waiting in the wings for his call. The Prince of Wales has at once a great part of his own to play in the drama of national history; but it is a part that he has largely to extemporize while already on the stage. The challenge is not new in his experience: he himself found that the position of the Guardian at Gordonstoun was very much what the individual incumbent had the desire and capacity to make of it. So also, on a loftier stage, is the great dignity of Prince of Wales.

What he will wish to make of it cannot be foreseen today, even by himself: if he knew how he would be thinking when he emerges from the university it would not be necessary to go there. Only the external, formal elements can be predicted.

King George VI used to say of the multitude of routine functions he and his wife and daughters had to perform: 'We're not a family; we're a firm.' The Prince of Wales cannot decline his responsibilities as an executive member of this hard-working company. Four years hence two of its busiest directors, Queen Elizabeth and the Duke of Gloucester, will both be seventy-two; they are entitled to take life more easily, and to see younger workers drafted into service at the other end of the age scale. The Prince of Wales is far the most important of these. His main duty in this domain is to relieve the direct burden of the Queen herself. She too lives under constant strain, and must often wish to delegate public responsibilities; but for most of these which are of truly national importance the only acceptable deputy is the future King.

As to his personal contribution, only a few things can be said. First, whatever new direction his thinking may take at Cambridge, it is certain that he will remain, in the Queen's phrase, 'a country person'. His love of the rural scene, of the home of his childhood at Balmoral and Sandringham, is ineradicable. His leisure life will inevitably shrink; but there is no doubt that for many years to come as much of it as possible will be devoted to his favourite sports of shooting, fishing, stalking and polo. In this he will be departing little from established royal family habit.

Secondly, there must within a few years come into existence what may be called a junior court. Just as the Queen as supreme representative of the nation has striven ceaselessly to make herself and her home familiar to the widest possible sections of her people, so the Prince of Wales, whether married or single, may be expected to make of his house a focus for influencing the young, whose representation is peculiarly vested in him. This influence is likely to reflect a new and distinctive personality. No British prince since the Stuarts has cared more sincerely for the things of the mind and the spirit. Mr. Geoffrey Dennis, contemplating the accession to the Throne of the last Prince of Wales, though he saw many hopeful omens, added one reservation: 'Unfortunately, among the young people of England Edward does not know the idealists.' The idealists are precisely the young people whom Prince Charles will take pains to know. In the outbreak of criticism of the monarchy in certain literary quarters about ten years ago, several writers complained that it did so little to encourage the arts. Once the Prince of Wales sets up his own establishment and gathers his junior court about him, he is likely to do much to remove that reproach.

Thirdly, and finally, he has a deep social conscience; or, to put it in less abstract and more human terms, a love of people and a keen desire to help them. His father has told him that the Royal Family, in National Insurance categories, count as 'self-employed', and must work to justify their keep. Prince Charles hardly needed that exhortation, for his desire to benefit humanity comes from within. Only, he has not yet the experience to perceive how best to give it expression. The future King Edward VIII made himself the missionary of Empire and Commonwealth, interpreting the many peoples under King George V's Crown to one another and maintaining the bonds between them. With the shrinkage of imperial responsibilities that can scarcely make a career for the present Prince. The future George VI chose as his special domain the welfare of workers in industry and the bridging of the gulf between the social classes. That work is largely done: there is no lack of bridges today. Prince Charles will require to find some new direction of princely activity for the common good, something that grows out of the needs of the modern world as it is, and as it is becoming. He belongs to that world, and, at the end of the thoughtful years on which he is about to embark, will be better able than his elders to judge how best it can be helped. He is no longer a child; it is to be hoped that he will be allowed to find his own answer to the principal question that overhangs his future. Whatever answer he gives, we may be confident that it will add something fresh to the connotation of his ancient motto '*Ich Dien*'—'I Serve'.

# PRINCES OF THE PAST

A THOUSAND YEARS of history lie behind the education of an heir to the British Throne.

Egbert of Wessex is traditionally regarded as the first King of all England—though this certainly exaggerates the authority of a ruler who spent most of his reign struggling to maintain himself at the same time against English rivals and invading Danes. He was a younger contemporary of the great Emperor Charlemagne, who laboured to achieve an intellectual revival in the Frankish lands, beginning in his own palace, and brought over an English scholar, Alcuin of York, to direct the movement. It is probable that with this example beyond the Channel some element of book-learning found its way into Egbert's family.

With Egbert's grandson, King Alfred the Great, we come for the first time on a figure that we can see as a living personality through the mists of a thousand years. It is difficult to say that any boy at that time was deliberately trained as a future king; for the law of primogeniture, securing the succession to the eldest son, did not take definitive shape for another three hundred years. On the death of a king the best available member of the Royal Family was put on the throne by the bishops and lay magnates. Alfred in fact had three elder brothers, each of whom reigned in turn before him; but he does seem to have been singled out very early in life as a prince with a future. When he was only four years old his father, King Ethelwulf, desperately beset by the Danes, sent the little boy under escort on a pilgrimage to Rome to implore divine protection. The Pope invested Alfred with the insignia of a Roman consul and sent him home to Winchester, where his education, together with his brothers, was taken in hand by his mother, Queen Osburh.[1]

1. The following account is given by his biographer, the priest Asser, who wrote while the great King was still alive:

'From his cradle a longing for wisdom before all things and among all the pursuits of this present life, combined with his noble birth, filled the noble temper of his mind; but alas, by the unworthy carelessness of his parents and tutors, he remained ignorant of letters until his twelfth year, or even longer. But he listened attentively to Saxon poems day and night, and hearing them often recited by others committed them to his retentive memory. A keen huntsman, he toiled unceasingly in every branch of hunting, and not in vain, for he was without equal in his skill and good fortune in that art, as also in all other gifts of God, as we have ourselves often seen.

'When therefore his mother one day was showing him and his brothers a certain book of Saxon poetry which she held in her hand, she said, "I will give this book to whichever of you can learn it most quickly." And moved by these words, or rather by divine inspiration, and attracted by the beauty of the initial letter of the book, Alfred said in reply to his mother, fore-stalling his brothers, his elders in years though not in grace: "Will you really give this book to one of us, to the one who can soonest understand and repeat it to you?" And, smiling and rejoicing, she confirmed it, saying: "To him will I give it." Then taking the book from her hand he immedi-ately went to his master, who read it. And when it was read, he went back to his mother and repeated it.

'After this he learnt . . . the services of the hours, and then certain psalms and many prayers. He collected these into one book . . . and was never parted from it. But alas, what he principally desired, the liberal arts, he did not obtain according to his wish, because, as he was wont to say, there were at that time no good scholars in all the kingdom of the West Saxons.

'He often affirmed with frequent laments and sighs from the bottom of his heart, that among all his difficulties and hindrances in this present life

In 887, when 'Wessex lay in a patch of peace Like a dog in a patch of sun', the King began to master the Latin language. Alfred was then about forty, and in the remaining twelve years of his life he himself made translations of several Latin standard works, adding commentaries of his own. He had in the meantime organized a school in his palace for the children of the nobility, and in it his son Edward and his daughter Aelfthryth were educated. In the school both Latin and English books were read, and Asser says that Edward and his sister were brought up with great care from their tutors and nurses.[1] Edward, known as the Elder, succeeded his father in 899, but we have no direct evidence for the next two centuries that any King of England, Anglo-Saxon, Danish or Norman, was able to read or write. Probably there was a great deal of oral instruction from bishops and eminent monks, alternating with strenuous military exercises. The principal recreations of young princes were hunting (the stag or the wild boar rather than the fox) and hawking, which came into fashion towards the end of the period.

Edward the Confessor was the first of the native-born Kings of England to be educated abroad. In 1013, when he was about eleven years old, the conquest of England by the Danish King Sweyn compelled his father, Ethelred the

this was the greatest: that, during the time when he had youth and leisure and aptitude for learning, he had no teachers; but when he was more advanced in years, he did have teachers and writers to some extent, when he was not able to study, because he was harassed, nay, rather, disturbed, day and night, both with illnesses unknown to all the physicians of this island, and with the cares of the royal office at home and abroad, and also with the invasions of pagans by land and sea.'

1. 'Nor, indeed, are they allowed to live idly and carelessly without a liberal education among the other occupations of this present life which are fitting for nobles: for they have learnt carefully psalms and Saxon books, and especially Saxon poems, and they frequently make use of books.'

Unready, to take refuge with Duke Richard II of Normandy; and although Ethelred himself enjoyed a brief restoration before his death in 1016, his son remained in Normandy throughout the reign of Sweyn's son, Cnut, and was a mature man when he was recalled to the throne in 1042. He appears to have been bilingual in French and English, and had acquired an interest in continental styles of architecture, which he applied in his foundation of Westminster Abbey (not, of course, the building that stands today). He has been credited with a cosmopolitan outlook, which perhaps means no more than the obvious fact that he knew two countries instead of one. But the court at Rouen did not afford a more sophisticated environment than that at Winchester. On the contrary, the Normans were only three generations away from their ferocious Viking past, and were at this time far behind the Anglo-Saxons in general culture.

Edward the Confessor was not an ancestor of Prince Charles (or of anybody else) though his successor, King Harold II, was. As for the great conqueror who defeated Harold at Hastings and seized his throne, it is difficult to imagine a childhood more certain, according to the ideas of modern psychology, to produce a juvenile delinquent. The least of his handicaps was that he was born illegitimate. In 1034, when he was only six, his father Duke Robert I set off on a pilgrimage to Jerusalem from which he never returned. Before departing he assembled the magnates of the Duchy of Normandy and persuaded them to take an oath of allegiance to the boy William as their Duke.

William was placed in the charge of Robert, Archbishop of Rouen, who was his great-uncle, Count Alan of Brittany, and a certain Turchetil the Paedagogue (destined to be the ancestor of the lords of Brecknock in Wales). But Robert died in 1037 and Alan in 1040; and then, says Professor David Douglas: 'his place as chief tutor was taken by

Gilbert the count . . . but within a few months Gilbert himself was murdered, when out riding, by assassins acting
under the orders of Ralph of Gace, one of the sons of Archbishop Robert. About the same time Turchetil was like-
wise assassinated. And Osbern Steward was killed at Vaud-
reuil after a scuffle in the very bedchamber of the boy duke.
William's household was in fact becoming a shambles, and
some idea of the conditions which had come to prevail
therein may be gathered from the story that Walter, the
brother of Herleve, was wont at this time to sleep in the
company of Duke William his nephew, and frequently at
night was forced to fly for safety with his charge to take
refuge in the cottages of the poor. It is not surprising that
these years left a lasting impression on the character of the
boy who was chiefly involved.'

Nor is it surprising that William never acquired anything
that the modern world regards as education. There is no
reason to suppose that he could read or write, or that he
ever learned any language but his own Norman French—
neither the Latin that was the universal language of culture,
nor the English of his future subjects.

Yet he profoundly respected the learning he himself had
never had the opportunity to acquire; and when his time of
power came he sent out for famous scholars and promoted
them to high place in England. Growing up in the midst of
a tangle of ferocious family feuds, there is small wonder that
he became hard, cruel and domineering. But he was also
shrewd, resolute and self-disciplined. He was plunged into
intestine warfare from early adolescence; at the age of nineteen, with the aid of the King of France, he won the great
victory of Val-es-Dunes against a coalition of his rebellious
vassals; and for the next thirteen years he was continually
fighting for mere survival. But he did survive; by 1060 he
had emerged master of Normandy, and would go on to be
master of England. Somehow his terrible childhood had

developed one of the commanding characters of history.

According to the Norman law and custom of the time, a father's inherited property passed to his eldest son, but anything he had himself added to his patrimony he was at liberty to dispose of as he would. So the Conqueror's eldest son, Robert Curthose, was brought up to be Duke of Normandy only. His next brother, William, was designated to succeed the Conqueror as King of England, and with that in view was placed for education in the household of Lanfranc, the great Italian-born scholar whom William had brought over from his abbey in Normandy to be Archbishop of Canterbury. The younger William, called Rufus from his red hair, did no credit to his pious upbringing. He cared nothing for books, only for hunting and military exercise. He was not only a homosexual; as King he became a notorious unbeliever and blasphemous scoffer at all Christian beliefs. It is a reasonable guess that in him (who has been called morally the worst of the English kings) we have a dreadful example of the danger of overdoing a good thing—that he had the Christian virtues so rammed down his throat in childhood that in adult life he reacted violently against the whole creed. But it is only fair to add that everything we know about him comes from the writings of churchmen, who never forgave him for quarrelling with Lanfranc's successor, the holy St. Anselm, and driving him into exile.

Of Rufus's brother, Henry I, Professor Galbraith writes: 'from his accession . . . dates the beginning of a new period in which kings can normally read, but do not, even if they can, write'. Henry was called in later tradition 'Beauclerk', which means 'accomplished scholar', but there is no evidence that he was given the nickname within two hundred years of his lifetime. He could probably read; and perhaps speak English as well as his native French.

Neither Stephen nor Maud was educated for the Throne, but with Maud's son, Henry, perhaps the greatest of the

Kings of England though certainly not an English king, we come with certainty to an educated monarch.[1]

But though Henry has been described as the perfect type of the literate layman of his age, there is no record of how he acquired his culture. His father, Geoffrey Plantagenet, Count of Anjou, was famous among the warrior princes of the age for his intellectual interests, but was so constantly away fighting that the child must have been left entirely to the care of his mother—something of a virago—until he was six years old. Then Geoffrey came home for three quieter years and put his son in the charge of a tutor called Master Pierre of Saintes, 'learned above all his contemporaries in the science of verse'. This presumably was the time when young Henry acquired the rudiments of book-learning, and with it the taste for study, which he retained through life. But in 1142, at the age of ten, he was sent off to England in the care of his uncle, Robert Earl of Gloucester, who was campaigning, with headquarters at Bristol, in support of Maud's claim to the throne. Here Henry was placed under one Master Matthew, to be 'imbued with letters and instructed in good manners, as beseemed a youth of his rank'. But it must have been a disturbed sort of education.[2] What he probably did

1. His friend Peter of Blois, in a letter to the Archbishop of Palermo, boasts of his master's superiority in learning to the King of Sicily, though he, who had been Peter's pupil, was considered a learned man; and the contemporary writer, Walter Map, says of Henry: 'he was inferior to none in bodily activity, lacking in no endeavour which another could perform, ignorant of nothing which befitted a gentleman, well learned for all the demands of social intercourse and practical affairs, having a knowledge of all the languages that are spoken from the Bay of Biscay to the Jordan [English, it will be noted, is not one of these], but making use only of Latin and French.'

2. As Kate Norgate writes, Bristol at that time 'fully kept up its character as "the stepmother of all England", he must have been continually seeing or hearing of bands of soldiers issuing from the castle to ravage and plunder, burn or slay, or troops of captives dragged in to linger in its dungeons till they had given up their uttermost farthing or were set free by a miserable death'.

learn from his uncle—who alone among the adventurers who had rallied to Maud's cause was qualified to teach it—was the new moral code of chivalry, which was now beginning to exercise its mollifying influence on the harsh manners of the feudal age. In 1147 he returned to the family circle at Angers; and Count Geoffrey handed over to him the Duchy of Normandy, which he had conquered from Stephen's adherents. Henry was fifteen, and according to Angevin ideas was to be reckoned an adult.

Richard I and John were younger sons, and so not brought up as future kings of England. Their eldest brother, Henry, known as 'the young king', had been crowned in his father's lifetime to make sure of the succession, but had rebelled against him and died young. By that time Richard and John were grown up, and Richard a semi-independent ruler as Duke of Aquitaine. Richard's whole interest was in his southern dominions and his crusade: he spent only eighteen months of his reign in England. But their mother, Queen Eleanor, and their half-sister, Marie de Champagne, were famous patrons of the new school of French lyrical poets, and they gew up in the atmosphere of that culture. Richard himself is known to have been a poet. John was almost certainly literate,[1] for he collected the first royal library, and there is extant a letter from him to the Abbot of Reading thanking him for a Latin book. Moreover he had for his tutor the learned Ranulf de Glanville, afterwards Chief Justiciar and reputed author of the first textbook of the Common Law.

John's son, Henry III, can scarcely be said to have had the

1. It is often pointed out that John did not 'sign' Magna Carta in the modern sense, but merely caused his Great Seal to be affixed to it. This is quite true, but has nothing to do with the question of his ability to write. The system of authenticating documents by writing one's name on them had not yet been invented; the most learned as well as the illiterate did it by attaching their seals (*signa* or *sigilla*), and that in 1215 was what 'signature' meant.

education of an heir to the Throne, for his father died when he was nine years old. He himself was a fugitive in the West Country; the French Prince who was afterwards to be Louis VIII held London and much of the eastern counties. The boy Henry was hastily crowned at Gloucester with 'a certain garland' belonging to his mother, because the Crown of St. Edward was in Louis's power at Westminster.

It was not till 1221, however, that Henry was crowned a second time in Westminster Abbey, and two years later, when he was sixteen, the Pope, then the feudal overlord of England, declared him to be old enough to take over the government. What sort of education he received during those first seven years, while others governed in his name, we do not know in detail. He seems to have been very much under the tutelage of William the Marshal, regarded for nearly half a century as the great prop of the Throne and the model of chivalry, and, after William's death in 1219, of his successor in the regency, Hubert de Burgh, Earl of Kent. From these two great men Henry would have had every opportunity to imbibe the ideals of knighthood. But it is not as a knightly figure that he is best remembered. A great influence upon the regencies was exerted by the legates residing in England as representatives of the papal overlord; and it was the Church, by declaring a crusade against the invading French, that had been largely responsible for his recovery of his capital.[1] So he grew up with an intense personal piety founded upon this sense of gratitude. One of the churchmen who did most to stimulate this devotion was the Archbishop of Canterbury, Cardinal Langton; and it was presumably from him that Henry acquired another of his

1. This certainly made a powerful impression on the boy king's mind. Long afterwards he wrote to Robert Grosseteste, the famous scholar-bishop of Lincoln: 'When we were bereft of our father in tender years, when our subjects were turned against us, it was our mother, the Holy Roman Church, that brought back our realm under our power, anointed us king, crowned us and placed us on the throne.'

abiding characteristics—his intense love of things English.

He was, of course, fundamentally a Frenchman, the grandson of Henry II who had come over from Anjou only sixty years before. But some genealogist had traced for him a descent from Alfred the Great, and this fired his imagination with patriotism for the land he had inherited. He dedicated himself to the memory of St. Edward the Confessor, the last king of the old Anglo-Saxon house; later on he was to give his sons the names of the two English royal saints, Edward and Edmund; and his great monument today is Westminster Abbey, which he rebuilt to provide a worthy shrine for St. Edward's bones. With this devotion to the English past went a feeling for architecture and the arts, for beauty of form in every department of daily life, for metalwork, for the detail of dress, decoration and ceremonial, which was something quite new in the line of heavy-handed warriors from which he came.

Henry and his wife Eleanor were particularly affectionate parents, and kept their son Edward, destined to be one of the greatest of English kings, close to themselves—contrary to the growing custom of the age, by which the sons of kings, as of lesser aspirants to chivalry, were sent to serve an apprenticeship in the household of some great nobleman. Instead Hugh Giffard, a Wiltshire baron, was brought to Windsor to take charge of the young Lord Edward until he was seven years old. The choice may have been dictated by the King's strong pious feelings, for Giffard was to become eventually the father of an archbishop, a bishop and two abbesses. With him perhaps the boy laid the foundation of the steadfast religious principles which made him the most faithful of husbands in an age when chastity was rare among princes, and a lavish benefactor of churches and monasteries (including Westminster Abbey)—with an unfortunate tendency to start ambitious foundations and then leave somebody else to raise the money to complete them.

Edward was a delicate child, and before he was eight contracted a dangerous illness at the foundation of Beaulieu Abbey. He was in danger for three weeks, during which the Queen, in defiance of the severe rules of the Cistercian Order, forced her way into the enclosure to nurse him. Nevertheless he grew up tall (he was nicknamed Long-shanks), strong and athletic. One weakness he did not over-come till much later in life, if ever—a pronounced stammer; but it did not prevent his becoming an eloquent speaker, not only in French but in English, although French was to re-main the language of the court and the ruling classes for at least a century after his time. That he was taught the langu-age of his future subjects is another piece of evidence show-ing his father's devotion to the Anglo-Saxon tradition. It is also known that Edward learned to read Latin, although there is little to show that he had more than an elementary capacity to write in any of his three languages. It was, how-ever, an age of great lawyers all over Europe, and in accord-ance with the fashion the heir was put through a thorough legal training, probably under Robert Burnell, who was later to serve him for seven years as Chancellor of the Realm.

Book learning, however, as with all the royalty and aristocracy of the age, took a secondary place in Edward's education to the acquisition of the accomplishments of chivalry. As an adolescent he was the chief of a little group of boys of royal blood, which included Henry, son of his uncle, Richard Earl of Cornwall, who when his father was elected King of the Romans became known as Henry of Almaine; the four sons of his Aunt Eleanor and her husband Simon de Montfort; and his young half-uncles of the House of Lusignan. In rivalry with these young companions he learned to be a first-class horseman, a passionate devotee of the chase, which still meant chiefly stag-hunting, an expert in falconry, and a keen competitor in the tournaments. He was only eight when his father started looking for a wife for him, and eventually, after years of negotiation, his mother took him off to Bordeaux in 1253, to be betrothed to the Infanta Eleanor, sister of Alfonso X, King of Castile. The marriage was solemnized later in the year, when Edward was fourteen. Directly afterwards, in accordance with the feudal custom called 'appanage', the King invested his son as lord of all Ireland (of which only a narrow strip called the Pale was really under English rule), the earldom of Chester, the king's lands in Wales, the islands of Jersey and Guernsey, the whole of Gascony, and the lands in France lost by John to which the English Crown still laid claim. This was the recognized way of training a future king in the art of government.

His early manhood was largely spent in civil war, and he grew up to be a hard and cruel, but a great and statesman-like king. He was serious-minded and conscientious and determined to bring up his sons in his own image. As has happened more than once in the history of the English kingship, they—or the one of them with whom we are here concerned—reacted strongly against their severe upbringing. His second son was born in Caernarvon Castle in 1284, when the King had just completed the conquest of Wales, in the course of which the great Llywelyn ap Gruffydd, who had for the first time united North and South Wales into a single principality, had been slain. But the later story that the King assembled the defeated Welsh chieftains at Caernarvon, promised they should have a new Prince who could 'speak not a word of English', and then produced his new-born son Edward, is pure invention. To the Welsh, rankling under defeat, such a gesture would have seemed only adding intolerable insult to injury; and if Edward ever made a joke in his life, it went unreported by contemporaries. Still more important, it is incredible that he should have bestowed so great a dominion on anyone but his eldest son and heir, Alfonso, Earl of Chester. Alfonso, however, died aged ten a few months later, so that Edward of Caernarvon was brought up as Heir Apparent to the Throne.

Before Alfonso died the baby Edward had moved on with his parents to Bristol, and he did not see Wales again until he was grown up. He spent a disturbed and restless childhood. His mother seems to have taken little interest in him, and died when he was six years old. Before and after that the royal nursery was a peripatetic affair, the young Lord Edward and his five sisters (no more boys were born) being carted about in the wake of the King in his constant journeyings to Wales, to the Scottish Border, and on frequent progresses about his English realm. When they became stationary for any length of time, it was usually at the royal manor of Langley in Hertfordshire, a place that young Edward learned to love. There he developed a marked taste for simple rural pursuits and rustic company. Nowadays we might think this was to his credit. Queen Elizabeth II, speaking of her eldest son, said, 'He's like the rest of our family; we are all country people'; and even in an urbanized age we are all pleased to know this of our future King. But in the mainly agricultural England of the late thirteenth century the men of weight at court did not look at it at all like that. When it was reported that the growing boy at Langley was amusing himself with hedging and ditching, helping the blacksmith at the forge and drinking ale with the household servants and local farmers, aristocratic hands were held up in horror.

These vulgar habits did not altogether prevent him from acquiring the conventional accomplishments of chivalry; he grew up 'fair of body and of great strength', could wield a lance dexterously and looked extremely well on a horse. But his heart was not in these things. He acquired a smattering of Latin from his tutors; he borrowed from Christ Church, Canterbury, Latin manuscripts of the lives of St. Anselm and St. Thomas which he never returned; and he is credited, though doubtfully, with the authorship of a melancholy poem in Norman French. But he was anything but a studious boy, neglecting his inevitably desultory lessons at every opportunity. His artistic tastes, which were pronounced, ran not to literature but to architecture, music and the theatre. This he no doubt inherited from his grandfather Henry III, without the vein of piety. His love of the theatre was such that when he became King he appointed as Treasurer of England one Walter Reynolds, whose only qualification is said to have been his dramatic genius—presumably as playwright rather than actor.

These aesthetic tastes were taken by the feudal nobility of the age, and indeed by the King, as evidence of effeminacy. It is the common charge of the soldier against the artist. Unfortunately in Edward's case the charge had some basis; for by the time he reached adolescence he had shown himself unmistakably homosexual. He is the third of the four Kings of England who have shown or suffered this perversion—the other three being William II, Richard I, and James I. Soon after his thirteenth birthday the King left him as nominal Regent of England while he himself visited his dominions in Gascony; and when he returned he brought back a young Gascon squire named Piers Gaveston, whom he attached to his son's household. Gaveston, said to have been the son of a witch, was brilliant, cultivated, frivolous and vicious; and young Edward fell in love with him. The unseemly intimacy between the two continued for the remaining ten years of Edward's life as heir; after his accession it brought Gaveston to the highest rank in the peerage and to a violent death on Blacklaw Hill; and the animosities it left behind had much to do with the eventual deposition of Edward himself and his dreadful end in Berkeley Castle.

Old King Edward Longshanks was no doubt prompted partly by anxiety about his son's unhealthy proclivities when he set about trying to find him a wife. He began when the child was only five, by proposing a marriage with the still younger Margaret the Maid of Norway, who had succeeded her grandfather Alexander III as Queen of Scots. But this match, which the King hoped would unite the kingdoms of England and Scotland, was thwarted by the death of the little bride at sea before she ever set foot on Scottish soil. King Edward then turned first to Flanders and afterwards to France, where at last he succeeded in negotiating a betrothal with Isabella, daughter of the mighty and terrible King Philip the Fair; but before the marriage could be celebrated he himself died. Before that, he had in effect proclaimed that the Lord Edward's years of tutelage were over by investing him in Parliament at Lincoln with all the royal lands in Wales, the earldom of Chester, the duchy of Aquitaine and the lordship of Ponthieu.

By this endowment young Edward was held to have become the successor of the great Llywelyn and, although the title of Prince was not included in the charter, he soon came to be known by it—the first member of the English royal house to be so designated. The lands assigned to him were not by any means the whole of Wales, nearly half of which had been long parcelled out among Norman barons called the lords of the March. What Edward received was that part of the country which had remained under native rule down to the conquest by his father. The date was February 7, 1301. Edward was seventeen years old. Six years later, on July 7, 1307, he became King Edward II.

The princes of the three generations that followed him all received the now conventional education of the sons of great lords in the heyday of chivalry.[1] Edward III grew up under

1. The routine was summed up by the rhyming chronicler, John Hardyng (1378–1465):

> 'And as lordes sonnes bene sette, at four yere age,
> To scole to lerne the doctryne of letture,
> And after at sex to have thaym in language,

this system to be a splendid and colourful figure in the chase, in the tournament and in war. His magnificence was somewhat superficial; his undoubted physical courage was matched with no more than mediocre generalship, and his intellectual capacity was no better than average. Such as it was, it was developed under the tuition of a great man, Richard Aungervyle, afterwards Bishop of Durham and Chancellor, author of a book-lover's encyclopaedia called *Philobiblion*. Some of this scholar's devotion to literature may have been remembered by his pupil, who as King was to take Chaucer and Froissart into his service. But it was his lay teachers of horsemanship and swordsmanship who made of young Edward the most spectacular of English kings.

His son Edward of Woodstock, called in later centuries but not in his own time the Black Prince, never became King. But he cannot be ignored, because with him originated most of the great English titles and dignities which have descended to Prince Charles. This was an age, not only of ostentatious pomp, but also of growing material opulence; and Edward III, in finding the customary feudal 'appanages'

> And sitte at mete semely in alle nurture;
> At ten and twelve to revelle in their cure,
> To daunse and synge, and speke of gentelnesse;
> At fourtene yere they shalle to felde I sure,
> At hunte the dere, and catch an hardynesse.
> . . . . . . . . . . . . .
>
> At sextene yere to werray and to wage,
> To just and ryde, and castels to assayle,
> . . . . . . . . . . . . .
>
> And every day his armure to assay
> In fete of armes with some of his meyne,
> His might to prove, and what that he do **may**
> Iff that he were in such a jupertee
> Of werre by falle, that by necessite
> He might algates with wapyns hym defende:
> Thus should he lerne in his priorite,
> His wapyns alle in armes to despende.'

for his son, was determined to endow him with wealth such as no heir to the Throne had enjoyed before. When the boy was three years old, in 1333, he conferred on him the earldom of Chester, with its four castles and its substantial revenues from certain lands in North Wales known as the Cantreds. Not long afterwards, the King's brother, John of Eltham, Earl of Cornwall, died without heirs; and at the age of seven young Edward received Cornwall also, now elevated in rank to become the first dukedom created in England. This great dignity was bestowed upon him during his father's lifetime, and thereafter upon 'the eldest sons of his heirs, Kings of England'. With it went a long list of castles and manors, not all of them in Cornwall, to which other property has been added in the course of the centuries. Ever since then the estates of the Duchy of Cornwall provide the income for the maintenance of the Heir Apparent and his establishment.

The third advancement of the young Edward, now thirteen, came on May 12, 1343, when the King in full Parliament invested him with the dignity of Prince of Wales. He himself had never borne this title, and it is from this date, rather than that of the investiture of Edward of Caernarvon in 1301, that the continuous history of the English Princes of Wales begins. It was now the firm intention that the principality should be the normal appanage of the Heir Apparent, although, unlike the dukedom of Cornwall which is entailed by charter, it waits to be conferred, with the earldom of Chester, at the Sovereign's pleasure. In the Black Prince's time it brought in revenues not much inferior to those of the Duchy, but this additional endowment has long since disappeared. The Principality also differs from the Duchy in that it can be conferred upon the Sovereign's grandson if his father (as in the reign of George II) is dead; but a Duke of Cornwall must be the Sovereign's son.

One more high honour was bestowed on the Black Prince

after he had 'won his spurs' at the age of sixteen in the battle of Crecy. There followed the siege of Calais, and the two Edwards returned in triumph to Windsor to set about realizing the King's treasured ambition of founding a Round Table like that of Arthurian legend. Exactly when the Order of the Garter was instituted is not certain; but most scholars now favour the year 1348.[1] It was to be dedicated to St. George, the patron of England, and to have its home at Windsor, where the Round Tower is said to mark the site of King Arthur's Table; and the knights were each to have a stall in the Chapel of St. George, which gradually took shape in the following century. The founder knights may well have been the participants in a great tournament at Windsor, in which the King contended with the Prince, each supported by a team of twelve; for to this day the stalls are allotted to the Sovereign and twelve knights on the south side of the Chapel and the Prince and twelve knights on the north. It is laid down in the statutes that the number of knights (apart from certain royal supernumeraries in modern times) is limited to twenty-four, not counting the reigning Sovereign and the Prince of Wales, who are declared to be constituent parts of the Order, even though the Prince may not yet have been dubbed knight and therefore cannot wear the robes or occupy his seat.

Two founder knights of the Order of the Garter were appointed by the Black Prince to take charge of the educa-

1. The story of its origin in the dropping of a garter by the Countess of Salisbury at a court ball, where the King picked it up with the words *Honi soit qui mal y pense*, was at one time discredited as an improbable fabrication of a later age, but more recent researches by Miss Margaret Galway (*University of Birmingham Historical Journal*, Vol. I, 1947), who has shown that the reference should be to Joan, Countess not of Salisbury but of Kent, have gone far to make it sound more probable. For Joan subsequently married the Prince of Wales himself, for whose special benefit the Order was founded. The ball may have taken place at Calais, where Countess Joan was present with the Queen during the siege; and the first assembly of the Order was probably the following year.

*Above:* Polo at Lilydale near Melbourne, January, 1966
*Previous page:* 'The Player-Prince': the dagger scene in
*Macbeth*, Gordonstoun, November, 1965

*Above:* On a Queensland cattle station, May, 1966
*Following pages:* Droving in Australia, May, 1966
A lifesaver's cap, at the Bondi Beach Carnival, Sydney

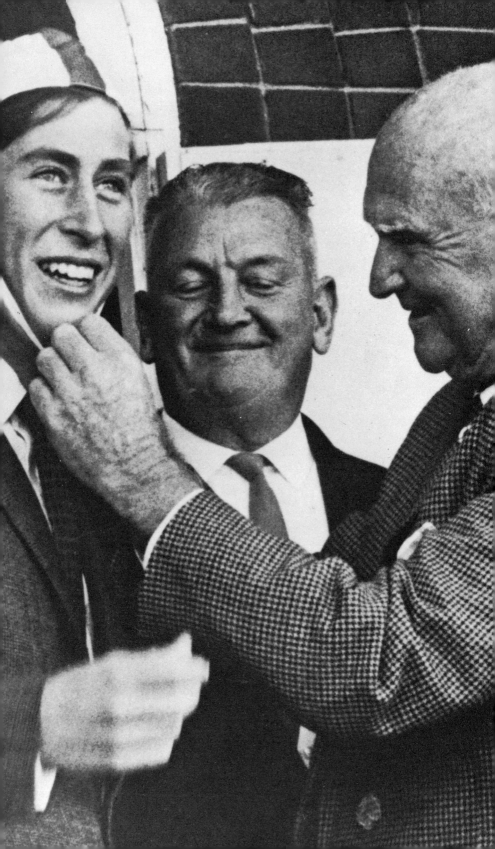

*Above:* In Trinity College dining hall with Robert
Woods, his neighbour in New Court, October, 1967
*Previous pages:* Inspecting a surf board at Bondi
A portrait by Godfrey Argent taken at Balmoral for the
Prince's 18th Birthday, November 14, 1966

tion of his only son, Richard, aged five, when he himself retired from the government of Gascony (where Richard 'of Bordeaux' was born) to spend the last years of his life as an invalid. The two were Guichard d'Angle, described by Froissart as a gentle knight, 'merry, true, amorous, sage, secret, large, prewe, hardy, adventurous and chivalrous', and Simon Burley, an old soldier, who possessed the remarkable library, for a layman, of twenty-one books, all but one of them in French, which was still, though not for much longer, the language of the court. But beyond the fact that Richard spent the next five years of his life at his mother's manor of Berkhamsted we have no record of his boyhood. It is presumed that the two knights followed the standard practice of the day, as laid down in the verse of John Hardyng[1]—reading at four, languages and good manners at six, dancing and singing at ten, and so on. It is exasperating that we know so little about the influences that formed the most complex character among our English kings, a character that fascinated Shakespeare and still fascinates audiences as interpreted by later dramatists. He may well have owed much to his warm-hearted wayward mother, Joan of Kent. Clearly he had the temperament of an artist rather than a statesman; set over an aristocracy avid of military glory he alienated most of them by his pursuit of peace; yet he was the son of the most famous soldier in Europe and showed that he inherited his father's spirit when, four years after becoming King at the age of ten, he rode out alone before the angry hosts of the Peasants' Revolt, who had just seen their chief, Wat Tyler, murdered, and proclaiming 'I will be your leader', led them away from threatened London.

Henry IV, the first King of the House of Lancaster, seized the Crown by force. If in any sense he was educated to be a king, it was as a future king not of England but of Castile, to whose throne his father, John of Gaunt, laid claim. But

1. See footnote to page 175.

the fortune of war in Spain went against John (though he always used the title King of Castile), and Henry in fact spent the latter half of Richard II's reign as a turbulent, and ultimately rebellious, participant in English politics. He found time to be a student of moral philosophy and a passionate devotee of music, and with his son, Henry of Monmouth, we come to the only King of England before Edward VII who can in a sense be called a university man.[1] But if Henry was ever an Oxford undergraduate, it can only have been for a few months in 1398. He was then twelve years old, not too young to begin university studies according to the ideas of the fourteenth century. He would presumably have made a start on what medieval teachers called the Trivium, consisting of Grammar, Rhetoric and Dialectic, which meant mainly reading, writing and arguing in the Latin language. In any case, he was not yet heir to the Throne, and his education as such can only be said to have lasted from October 1399, when he was made Prince of Wales and Duke of Cornwall (and next month Duke of Lancaster and Aquitaine) and July 1403, when he was wounded at the battle of Shrewsbury, leading his father's troops to victory over Henry Percy called Hotspur.

Until the rebellion of the Percies he himself had been in the guardianship of Hotspur's father, the Earl of Northumberland, whose support had been the principal factor in the successful rebellion that brought Henry IV to the Throne. Exactly how he was trained in that great household we do not know. But such accounts as we have of his youth give a picture curiously unlike the popular reputation of the victor of Shrewsbury, Harfleur and Agincourt. He was something of an athlete: 'a runner and a jumper, but not a hunter'. But,

1. The rooms (now demolished) over the main gate of Queen's College in which the young Prince had resided under the care of his uncle Cardinal Beaufort, then Chancellor of the university, were long pointed out. The evidence is not quite conclusive, but Dr. A. B. Emden, editor of the ancient Oxford registers, records it as probably true.

according to a French observer when he was already King,
though he had the fine manner of a lord and a noble stature,
he seemed more suited to the Church than to war. This is
not a unique judgment. According to the evidence of many
contemporaries, Henry V acquired somewhere in his upbringing—could it have been in those impressionable
months at Oxford?—a piety, almost a sanctimoniousness,
unknown in the royal family since his ancestor Henry III.
In all his campaigning for the conquest of France he believed
himself to be contending for the purposes of God, and his
defeated adversary to be undergoing punishment for resist-
ance to the divine will.

From his youth up, says Professor Jacob, our best living
authority on his reign, 'interest in moral and theological
questions never left him. His consultation of recluses, his
visits to shrines, his refusal to be interrupted even by his
magnates during the course of divine service, his zeal for the
purity of the Benedictine Order, his final hope to recover
Jerusalem, are facets of a predominantly clerical nature,
signs that he took the sacring at his coronation more
seriously than his predecessors, and that for him the prestige
and success of his country were connected with the moral
and religious qualities of the monarchy.'

All this is a little hard to reconcile with the picture we
know best of the revellings at the Boar's Head tavern with
Falstaff, Bardolph and Nym, and of the other traditions of
running amok with these boon companions in the London
streets, and being imprisoned by the Chief Justice himself
—whom afterwards as King he is said to have magnani-
mously complimented on his refusal to be overawed by his
future Sovereign. The traditions go back a long way, and
there may have been some outbreaks of wildness to justify
them. They relate in any case to a period when Henry was
of a more mature age than the present Prince of Wales has
yet reached, and can be cited neither as a precedent nor as a

warning as Prince Charles begins his undergraduate career. In so far as they are incompatible with the testimony to Henry's religiosity, it is the testimony that must be preferred—a little to the writer's unregenerate regret. 'Dramatic figments,' says Dr. Jacob again, 'such as the Boar's Head tavern, with all its engaging scallywags, will have to go.' There may have been a sudden steadying with the coming of supreme responsibility; but Holinshed goes rather far in representing Henry at his accession as suddenly 'washed in the laver of repentance and decently adorned in the garment of virtue'.

Under the Treaty of Troyes, which sealed the victory of Agincourt, Henry V married Catherine of Valois, daughter of the King of France, and he or his heir was to succeed to the French throne when Charles VI should die. The only child of the marriage, another Henry, was born on December 6, 1421. On August 31, 1422, Henry of England died, and on October 11 the same year Charles of France followed him to the grave. Thus when he was barely ten months old the baby Henry VI found himself King both of England and of France.

Setting aside the will of Henry V, which had made other provisions, the magnates of the realm assumed authority and arrangements were made for regencies in both kingdoms. By the common law of England the Sovereign is always of age. Accordingly, in the letters patent that shortly passed the Great Seal, it is 'We, Henry, by the Grace of God, etc.' who appoint our beloved uncle, John, Duke of Bedford, to be Protector of France and our other dear uncle, Humphrey, Duke of Gloucester, to be Protector of England. 'We' even appoint one Alice Butler to be our nurse, 'with licence reasonably to chastise Us in case of need'. Above Dame Alice the Duke of Gloucester was to have responsibility for the royal person. The King, however, remained in the household of his mother, Queen Catherine, who brought him at once to Westminster for the lords to do their homage and fealty to him, and later supported him on the Throne at the opening of the October Parliament of 1423, when he was nearly two years old.

When he was eight his dominions in France began to disintegrate. Joan of Arc, having triumphantly raised the siege of Orleans and seen the English army broken in the battle of Patay, pushed on to Rheims and there procured the coronation of the Dauphin as Charles VII. A counter-stroke on the same high spiritual plane was urgently necessary; the boy King Henry was hurried across the Channel to be himself crowned King of France. Rheims Cathedral, the traditional sacring place ever since the time of Clovis, the first Christian King a thousand years before, was in the hands of the enemy. The English settled for the next best thing; a coronation performed by the Bishop of Paris in Notre-Dame. But the hope that with this mystical grace upon him the child would win the loyalty at least of the Parisians was not realized. He was brought back to Windsor, not to see France again till he took refuge there in exile as a middle-aged man. The tide of the Hundred Years War continued to flow against his generals, though the last English army did not surrender until 1453.

Alone of the medieval Kings of England, Henry VI never acquired the military accomplishments of chivalry. Nor did he have any intellectual distinction. His blood bore the fatal taint of his French grandfather, Charles VI, who had died insane; and he himself was to be afflicted in the same way from his early thirties onwards. His mental weakness was in fact apparent in his boyhood. He was destined all his life to be a pawn in the hands of others, carted about like part of the baggage to the battlefields of the Wars of the Roses under the domination of his masterful wife, and, before his marriage, tossed to and fro between the parties of his undisciplined uncles. Yet he was a lovable character, gentle, magnanimous and holy—so holy that there is still a movement among historically minded English Catholics to procure his canonization as a saint.

His uncle Humphrey of Gloucester was a baleful influence in English politics, but has an honourable place in the history of English culture.[1] Under his auspices, though not at his hands, King Henry became as cultivated a man as his moderate intellectual equipment permitted; and the sense of values that he acquired in his youth was expressed in the magnificent foundations he left to posterity. King's College, Cambridge; All Souls College, Oxford; and Eton College across the river from his own Windsor, ensure that the memory of this apparently passive King will honourably survive the fame of all the proud baronial swordsmen who treated him in his lifetime with such disdain.[2] Henry VI must be accounted the most pathetic of English Kings, where Charles I is the most tragic.

Neither Edward IV, the first of the Yorkist Kings, nor Richard III was reared with any firm prospect of succession to the Throne, and Edward V, deposed as illegitimate after a few weeks of nominal reign and later probably murdered in the Tower, was never effectively King. When Richard, last of his line because his only son died young, fell at Bosworth on August 21, 1485, there ended (as G. K. Chesterton put it) 'the War of the Usurpers; and the last and most doubtful of all the usurpers, a wanderer from the

1. In the last generation before the introduction of printing revolutionized education the Duke of Gloucester was a mighty collector of books and patron of learning; he was the principal founder of what afterwards became the Bodleian Library at Oxford, and its most beautiful reading room is still known as Duke Humphrey's.

2. He also provided for the kingly education of his son, Edward Prince of Wales, by causing his Chief Justice, Sir John Fortescue, to write a book on *The Governance of England* expressly for his instruction. Edward was killed at the battle of Tewkesbury before he could read it—but the book remains a standard authority for students of history in English universities.

Welsh marches, a knight from nowhere, found the crown of England under a bush of thorn'. The wanderer became Henry VII.

It is one of the minor ironies of history that, of the five Sovereigns of the Welsh House of Tudor, only one was ever Prince of Wales: the second son of the victor of Bosworth, the Lord Henry, who eventually succeeded as King Henry VIII. He did not become Prince of Wales until he was eleven years old, for his elder brother Arthur lived until 1502. But the two boys, so far as the four-year interval between their ages permitted, were educated together and shared the same tutor while Arthur lived. Both, in their father's mind, were to be fitted for great place.[1]

Caxton's printing press had been set up in Westminster, so that new ideas became much more rapidly disseminated through the educated class. Scholars were exploring the Greek and Latin classics afresh for their aesthetic rather than their philosophical values. This wind of humanism blew chiefly from Italy, whose enlightened despots welcomed Greek men of letters and scientists to their courts, and where such potentates as Pope Pius II were notable leaders of the movement. In England its first effects were felt in the university of Cambridge, which was a little readier than Oxford to welcome the new ideas, and consequently rose in this period for the first time to equal prestige with the older university and soon began to exert the predominant intellectual influence in Church and State.

The tutor chosen by Henry VII to take charge of his young sons was a Cambridge man, John Skelton, whose qualifications bridged the transition between the old learning of the scholastics and the new culture of the humanists.

1. It is said that his intention was that Henry—whom he made Duke of York and Earl Marshal of England at the age of three—should become Archbishop of Canterbury. With our hindsight over his later career that would have been a singular appointment in an age when the celibacy of the clergy was still unchallenged.

Though destined to be speedily overshadowed by the flowering of lyrical poetry in the next generation, he was the only notable poet England had produced since Chaucer. He composed his own moral treatise for the instruction of his royal pupils, and historians of Henry VIII's reign have often quoted the passage in which Skelton admonishes the ideal prince to 'Cultivate sobriety and self-restraint. Avoid drunkenness. Eschew luxury. Shun the company of lewd women. Defile not your marriage.'

Under Skelton's tuition young Henry became probably the best Latin scholar the English Royal Family had ever known. Latin was still the language of diplomacy; Henry as a boy could carry on a correspondence in it with Erasmus and as King could converse easily with the ambassadors accredited to his court. He was equally fluent in French, could make a good showing in Italian, and seems in his boyhood to have shown some aptitude for mathematics.

Having been taught in his most impressionable years by a poet, Henry was by no means a contemptible poet himself. He showed great enthusiasm for music and was a composer of both liturgical and lyrical melodies. And, until he grew unwholesomely fat in middle age, he was an outstanding athlete—a tennis player, an archer, and a jouster who could compete on better than equal terms with the most brilliant young men about the court.

By the time Henry VIII had to consider the education of his own children humanism had triumphed all along the line. Both Greek and Latin were the indispensable staple of education, and all other subjects had to take a subsidiary place. But the Royal Family was now exposed to the conflicts not of the Renaissance but of the Reformation. The Lady Mary, daughter of the inflexibly Catholic Catherine of Aragon, was brought up mainly by her mother, and the King, still hoping for a male heir, took little interest in her. The Lady Elizabeth, who was declared illegitimate at the

[ 186 ]

age of three when her mother was condemned and exe-
cuted, spent a precarious childhood, menaced by the ebb
and flow of the religious factions at court. The Lord
Edward, Duke of Cornwall (who was never made Prince
of Wales), being younger than his two half-sisters, spent the
most important years of his boyhood under the influence of
his uncles the Seymours, friendly to continental Protestant-
ism.

Both girls began lessons at four. Catherine of Aragon sent
to her native Spain for one of the most famous living theo-
rists on education, Luis Vives, who came to England and
was installed as a fellow of Corpus Christi College, Oxford.
This was a new foundation, and the first home in Oxford
of Greek learning. Here Vives composed a series of studies,
in Latin, on female education: *The Instruction of a Christian
Woman*, *A Plan of Study for Girls*, and *The Bodyguard*. The
first two were dedicated to Queen Catherine, the last to the
Lady Mary. The still more famous Dr. Thomas Linacre of
All Souls, founder of the Royal College of Physicians, trans-
lated his own Latin grammar especially for her use. A series
of great ladies were appointed her governesses, and under
their direction the teachings of Vives, Linacre and other
great authorities were applied by specialist tutors of lesser
rank. The lessons continued uninterrupted when Mary,
aged nine, with the Countess of Salisbury as governess, took
up her residence at Ludlow Castle as titular head of the
Council by which Wales was administered.[1]

By that time she was able to reply in Latin to a compli-
mentary address from a commercial delegation; and a few
years later she could converse with equal facility in Latin,
French and Italian; Spanish she had spoken with her mother

1. It is not true, as some historians have stated, that the title of Princess
of Wales was ever conferred upon her. It can never be given to a woman,
for the effect might be, and in this case would have been, to deprive an
unborn male heir of his birthright.

almost from babyhood. She was still devoting most of her time to study at the age of twenty, dividing her day into three equal parts, one for the scriptures, one for languages (including by this time Greek), and the last for music. She had played the virginals since she was three, and was now also learning the lute. Her religious instruction she probably derived almost insensibly from Queen Catherine and the chaplains attached to her household. It is clear that her mind was fixed in an inflexible devotion to the Catholic faith. She herself probably regarded this as the only element of her education that mattered.

Erudite as Mary appears by the standards of our less scholarly age, she was quite outdone by both the younger children of Henry VIII. Tutors of high academic standing at Cambridge were procured for both of them: for Elizabeth the versatile Roger Ascham, author of *The Schoolmaster* and also of the standard textbook of archery; for Edward, the Regius Professor of Greek, John Cheke. Since there were only three years between their ages, each received a certain amount of instruction from the other's tutor, assisted by subordinates teaching modern languages and arts. Elizabeth was writing letters in Italian by the time she was eleven; she was thoroughly instructed in Greek, both the classical language of the great dramatists and historians and the Hellenistic in which she read the New Testament; she could reply extempore in Latin to formal addresses; she habitually talked in their own tongues to the French, Italian and Spanish Ambassadors. In addition she had learned from Ascham, a famous calligrapher, an exquisite handwriting, and could play on the lute and virginals, and dance even in old age to the music of others, as the peer of anyone in her brilliant court.

Her younger half-brother, Edward, who had superseded both princesses as heir to the Throne, was given a similar education; but by the time he was three Protestant influ-

ences had become powerful at court and the teachers
assembled for him round Cheke were all of 'the reforming
persuasion'. He grew up as an infant prodigy, and nearly as
much of a bigot on one side of the religious controversy as
Mary on the other. He became King when only ten years
old; but continued his lessons under Cheke until he died at
the age of sixteen. Every effort was made to train him in the
athletic and military skills which had been considered essential for a prince since feudal times, but his physical frailty
made proficiency impossible. His intellectual attainments,
on the other hand, were staggering. In his short life he seems
to have read all the great body of classical literature that
Elizabeth read in her whole course of education, translating
at least one Greek book complete into Latin; and in addition
he was drilled in the latest Protestant dogmas in the ponderous Latin of the German theologian Melanchthon.[1] He even
acquired some knowledge of astronomy, which implies
substantial skill in mathematics.

The Renaissance came later to Scotland than to England,
but by 1567, when the tragic Queen Mary was forced to
abdicate and take refuge in England, leaving her son James,
born the previous year, as nominal King, the dedicated
scholars in whom the country has always abounded were
grasping the new learning with enthusiasm. The baby was
placed in the care of the Earl and Countess of Mar, while
the Lords of the Council devoted their collective wisdom
to planning his education. History records few more violent
and self-seeking oligarchies than the Scottish nobility at this
particular epoch; but in their care for their Sovereign's welfare they seem to have done their honest best according to
their lights. These were not the lights of modern psycho-

1. 'At fourteen', writes Mr. Morris Marples, whose *Princes in the
Making* is a mine of information for the later part of this chapter, 'he had
reached a standard in languages, though not one must emphasize in anything else, comparable with that of Oxford and Cambridge open scholarship candidates today.'

logy, which might have expected the poor child to collapse under the sheer weight of learning imposed upon him. Eight or nine tutors, including musicians and riding masters, were assembled to devote their whole time to teaching the boy. At their head was the greatest scholar in Scotland, George Buchanan, a Latinist of European reputation even in that erudite age. With him was a much younger man, Peter Young, afterwards the historian of his country, who had the great advantage in the eyes of the lords that he had been trained in Calvin's Geneva and could be trusted to eradicate all hereditary tendency to the Popish principles of the deposed Queen.

Under the discipline of this formidable junta the child had his nose kept to the grindstone for perhaps twelve hours a day, being summoned from time to time from the school-room to don his robes of state and preside at some royal function. He acquired much the same linguistic accomplishments as his Tudor cousins, but his range of scholarship was wider. In particular, no doubt under the influence of Young, he gained a wide knowledge of modern history.

He was an apt pupil at absorbing facts; but there was a vein of obstinacy in him, perhaps inherited from his mother, which resisted the inculcation of opinions. He did not adopt the dearest principles of his teachers; on the contrary, he reacted strongly against them. To the austere teaching of Calvinist Presbyterianism, hammered into him by Young and others, James VI of Scotland was bound to submit; but later, when he was released from pressure as James I of England, his maxim was 'no bishop, no king', and he became the advocate of the Anglican 'middle way'. Buchanan had been resolute in the medieval political philosophy, which holds that the Law is from God and kings are subject to the law, but James had had enough of subjection, and followed the new doctrine, which he maintained with considerable learning, of the Divine Right of Kings. From the point of view of those who had wished to shape him to their own ideal, he is a notable object-lesson in the un-wisdom of driving a willing horse (which intellectually he was) too hard.

Besides his learning he had one polite accomplishment— he wrote and even published poetry. It is mediocre stuff, but it stands to his credit that he later gave his royal patronage to a better poet than himself, William Shakespeare. But the other graces of a Renaissance prince, in music and the arts, were unknown to him. His person was uncouth and his manners coarse. Nor was he anything of an athlete, though a good horseman. His qualification for kingship rests almost entirely on his book learning, which was wide, genuine and founded on a real love of the things of the mind.[1]

He wrote a manual of instruction for princes called *Basilikon Doron* (Kingly Gift), intended as a textbook for his elder son Henry, Prince of Wales. Henry died at the age of eighteen in 1612, and his younger brother Charles, Duke of York, became the new heir at the age of twelve. Up to that time there had been no question of giving him an education designed to fit him for the Throne. At his birth, in Scotland, he had been reported 'a very weak child'; he was small, his legs in his first few years would scarcely support him, and he was afflicted with a stammer that caused him lifelong embarrassment. His father, and later his brilliant elder brother, had decided that there was no future for him in secular life, and that he had better be educated for the post of Archbishop of Canterbury. (The same suggestion was made for the future Henry VIII, with whom Charles shares a grave at Windsor.) It was perhaps because of this bias in his early training that the new Prince of Wales remained the

1. He may have been something of a pedant; but the description of him as 'the wisest fool in Christendom' is that of contemporary malice. Professor Trevor Roper is more fair in calling him 'an omniscient umpire, whom no-one consulted'.

most devout adherent of the Church of England and probably lost his life because he refused to agree to its dis-
establishment.

It stands to Charles's credit that he overcame the physical
disability with which he had been born. As a boy he threw
himself into the strenuous sports in which his brother
excelled. He was constantly in the saddle, hunting and tilting
at the ring (an exercise equivalent to the modern 'tent-
pegging'); he took up tennis with a professional to instruct
him; and he became an addict of golf, which was to remain
his pastime to the end of his life. By the time he became
Prince of Wales the apparent cripple had developed—though
little of stature—into an upstanding and athletic boy.

On the academic side he was placed under the tuition of
Peter Young, now an elderly man, who had taught both his
father and his brother. Beyond that, nothing is certain. The
regime was probably a good deal less bookish than it had
been with the Tudors, or with King James under Buchanan's
direction; but certainly Charles was deeply affected by his
father's notions of paternal government, founded upon the
dogma of the Divine Right of Kings. The clash between
these principles and the parliamentary theory of the Common Law, linked with Puritan theology, makes the tragic
history of his reign. On the other hand his fastidious manners and profound feeling for the arts, which made him the
principal founder of the great royal collections of today,
plainly derive from sheer revulsion against the uncouth
court of King James.

With his son, who was to become Charles II, the standards of royal education continued their slow decline. Civil
war broke over England when this Charles was nearly
twelve; and the first hostilities on the Scottish border had
begun about the time when he was given his own establishment as Prince of Wales at the age of eight. He was then
placed in the charge of the Marquess (afterwards Duke) of

Newcastle, while the actual teaching was supervised by Brian Duppa, who after holding various appointments at Oxford died Bishop of Winchester. Charles developed a lifelong respect and affection for Duppa, but it was Newcastle who exercised the greater influence on his development. The Marquess was very much a man of the world, and depreciated book learning in comparison with the accomplishments of the courtier and the man of action. This was teaching very much in accord with Charles's temperament, inherited much less from his scholarly father than from his frivolous but gallant mother, Henrietta Maria. Duppa did his best, but the Prince never mastered the elements of Latin, in an age when Latin scholarship was the key to everything of value in education. Once war had broken out, and the Prince was following his father's fortunes from one besieged or threatened headquarters to another, the teaching became ever more haphazard; and when final defeat sent him into exile at fifteen it ended altogether. As Newcastle would have wished, he learnt in a bitter school to know men rather than books. If ever a king was educated in the school of life, this was he.

Charles II was the last child to be brought up as a future Sovereign in England for nearly a hundred years. He had no legitimate child; his brother James was only accepted as heir with the utmost reluctance (because of his religion) when he was over fifty. James in his turn was driven into exile with his infant son, and never returned; William III, who supplanted him, had been educated in his native Netherlands, and James's daughters, Mary II and Anne, were never contemplated as Queens until they were mature women. George I 'in pudding time came o'er' from Hanover, bringing his grown-up son with him to be Prince of Wales; both were Germans through and through and it was much too late for any teacher to attempt to make Englishmen of them. Not till 1738 was another prince born within the realm who was destined to succeed to the British Throne.

King George II's eldest son, Frederick—'poor Fred, who was alive and is dead'—is the most insignificant figure in the long line of the Princes of Wales. But he had one flash of insight into fundamentals. Though he himself had been brought up as a German in Hanover, he was the first of his family to grasp that a future King of England ought to be educated as an Englishman. It was too late to do anything about himself, but he made that the deliberate object of the upbringing he planned for his own eldest son, George. He wished his heir, as his political testament says, to be 'not only an Englishman born and bred but by inclination'.

George and his brothers were given a succession of governors, and each governor was supported by a tutor who arranged the course of studies. These studies, under mathematics masters, classics masters, teachers of fencing, dancing, music and other accomplishments then thought important for an English gentleman, occupied four and a half hours every morning and three and a half most afternoons. The trouble was that the governors and tutors were apt to be changed in an arbitrary way according to the fluctuating balance of parties, or the factions within the Whig party, in Parliament.

There was a specially sharp break when Frederick died in 1751 and George, at the age of thirteen, succeeded his father as Prince of Wales. The Duke of Newcastle's ministry installed a group of four preceptors, headed by Lord Harcourt, with a clear commission to see that the next King should grow up in harmony with their principles. The four, however, were soon at loggerheads with one another. At the same time the widowed Princess of Wales was exercising a considerable influence on her son's mind, handing on to him that bitter antipathy to parental influence which had been felt by Frederick for his father and was almost universal in the Hanoverian family. Thus the boy was in frequent revolt against his aging grandfather, George II, who, even when he was seventeen, once lost his temper and thrashed him with his own royal hands.

The breach was widened on a more intellectual plane when the Princess fell under the spell of Henry St. John, Viscount Bolingbroke, author of *The Patriot King*. This work, introduced by Augusta, Princess of Wales, to her young son, became his political manual, and from it he imbibed something of the old Tory outlook to set against the High Whig dogma which had gone practically un-challenged since 1714. To the Whigs the government of the realm was the natural perquisite and responsibility of the greater landed aristocracy, and the purpose of the monarchy was simply to register their decisions and give them formal authority. Bolingbroke conceived of the King as the supreme arbiter, above and detached from all parties and all classes, able by his inherent authority to speak over the heads of the aristocracy directly to his people.

The effect of this teaching on young George was re-doubled when his mother took the brilliant and debonair John Stuart, third Earl of Bute, as her political ally.[1] Bute also took his philosophy from Bolingbroke's writings; so that when the old King died in 1760 George III promptly installed Bute as his Prime Minister—the first Scot to hold that office in the United Kingdom—and proclaimed his intention to reign as the Patriot King by declaring in his first Speech from the Throne that he gloried in the name of Britain (or Briton).

At that date his mind had become fixed in the political opinions he was to profess as King; but his schoolroom studies do not seem to have progressed very far. He was eleven before he could read English (which was his natural

1. Popular scandal assumed the alliance to go far beyond the political; but this is not proved, though many of the best informed contemporaries, including Horace Walpole, believed the worst.

language), though he had a good conversational knowledge of both German and French. One of his last tutors in his final report wrote that the Prince of Wales was 'averse from work, indifferent to pleasure, usually in a state of total inaction and for practical purposes still in the nursery'.

George IV, as much cleverer than his father as he was morally less worthy, was educated on much the same lines. As usual in the Hanoverian family he was generally at odds with the King; indeed he afterwards said that his father had hated him ever since he was seven. In a century when Cabinets were still largely chosen by the Sovereign, and no Government that went to the polls with his blessing ever lost a general election, politicians out of office were accustomed to gather round the heir in the expectation that his accession to the Throne would bring them to power. They naturally found it to their interest to fan any spark of dissension between father and son. Personal incompatibility between governor and tutor, with appeals from one or the other to the King, caused several dismissals; but on the whole the regimen proceeded rather more smoothly than in the previous reign. George III may have disliked his heir, but he wanted to be proud of him and of the twelve brothers and sisters who made up the huge Royal Family. So noblemen of high rank served as governors, and important prelates as tutors. The most eminent of these was William Markham, Bishop of Chester, who later became Archbishop of York. He had been headmaster of Westminster, which in the eighteenth century was by far the most successful of the public schools in the production of Prime Ministers and other statesmen; and, taking charge of the Prince of Wales at the age of nine, he had orders from the King to treat him just as he had done his Westminster schoolboys, and to flog him whenever he deserved it.

Later on, when young George was sixteen, he and his brother Frederick, Duke of York (the later commander-in-chief), were set up in a house on Kew Green in the company of their tutor, Richard Hurd, Bishop of Worcester. Their four brothers were similarly accommodated, with tutors of their own, in two other houses on the Green, so that the whole set-up was almost a miniature of the 'house' organization of a public school in later days. Although George was probably quite as idle a pupil as his father had ever been, he acquired enough scholarship to bandy Greek and Latin tags with his more accomplished friends. Command of modern languages was also fashionable and he seems to have learned from his Swiss tutor, M. de Suizas, all three of the languages, French, German and Italian, which were spoken in the cantons. He read poetry and had an individual and ebullient taste in architecture (the Brighton Pavilion is his most characteristic monument). Without being in any sense learned he has some claim to be considered the most cultivated heir to the Throne since Charles I.[1]

He is also the only Prince of Wales to have reigned in that rank over Great Britain and her Empire; for during the last nine years of his father's life (and informally for a few months in 1788–9) he was installed as Regent while the old

1. Beginning his lifelong pursuit of women, all older than himself, at fifteen, he may also be considered the most scandalous since Henry V (if indeed the scandalous stories about Henry, which were of a different character, are true). Sir Llewellyn Woodward sums him up as 'a clever, versatile, lazy man, of some taste in architecture and painting, attractive and rude by turns, but always a liar, always selfish, bad in his private and public conduct, and without the least understanding of his age. He was a fair judge of character, but he never used his judgment for the good of the state, and never concerned himself with anything which did not, ultimately, affect his own pleasure.'

Bishop Hurd, when the Prince was fifteen, expected him to become 'either the most polished gentleman or the most accomplished blackguard in Europe—possibly both'.

George had the saving grace to acknowledge his own failings. Contemplating the education of his daughter Princess Charlotte, he wrote: 'Above all, I must teach her to speak the truth; you know that I don't speak the truth and that my brothers don't.'

King was secluded at Windsor, suffering from a malady of the mind for which the contemporary diagnosis of madness has been disputed by recent medical writers.

George IV's brother, William IV, had ten children by his mistress but none by his wife. The Crown passed to Victoria, who came to the Throne at the age of eighteen as the most ignorant Sovereign since the Middle Ages. She herself, looking back on her youth from the standpoint of her widowhood, thought that she had received her true education from her husband; and there is no reason to doubt it, for his very able brain had been highly developed by his German instructors, and the royal couple settled down after their marriage, in the earnest manner of the coming Victorian age, to long courses of serious reading and self-improvement. As princess her life had consisted of thirteen years in almost nun-like seclusion with her mother at Kensington Palace, followed by five in which frequent court appearances, under rigid chaperonage, as heiress presumptive to her uncle William IV continually distracted her attention from the perfunctory lessons arranged for her.

In that first phase of thirteen years the young princess lived in an overwhelmingly German environment. Her mother, who at her birth had been only about a year away from her native Saxe-Coburg, scarcely spoke any English. Baroness Lehzen, her governess from the age of five, was a Hanoverian, and normally conversed with her pupil in German. This lady, harsh, ugly and narrow-minded, was the dominant influence in forming Victoria's mind; though she said that she had never seen such a passionate and naughty child, a deep and lasting affection was formed between them so that in the first years of the reign, at any rate till the Queen's marriage, Lehzen was accounted one of the great powers behind the throne. Under her general direction male teachers were brought in to deal with the subjects of which they had special knowledge, notably Dr. Davys,

Dean of Chester, who failed to implant in the young mind
even an elementary knowledge of Latin, but led her more
effectively through the Bible and the more ponderous
English classics, and she developed a special interest in
history.

Though the confined Kensington environment ensured
that she remained intellectually backward, young Princess
Victoria excelled in the accomplishments that her age considered more appropriate than scholarship to a well-bred
girl. She was taught drawing, calligraphy and dancing by
experts, and taught well. Landscape drawing became one of
the relaxations of her middle life; she danced beautifully as a
girl and, when at last she resumed some sort of social life
after her long seclusion in widowhood, she surprised a
younger generation by showing that she retained the gift
at seventy. She learned to play several musical instruments,
and took professional lessons to train her naturally good
singing voice.

In the last years of King William's life King Leopold of
the Belgians, brother of the Duchess of Kent, sent over one
of his own trusted servants, Baron Stockmar, a Swede by
descent and a doctor by early training, who exercised an
even stronger influence than Lehzen upon the mind of
Queen Victoria and almost as much on that of her Consort.
Whatever understanding of politics the new Queen possessed on her accession in 1837 was derived mainly from him
and from the studies of English constitutional history in
which he guided her.

Earnestly as Queen Victoria and Prince Albert laboured
to educate themselves, they expended even more energy on
planning for the education of their eldest son. Stockmar
advised: the Prince directed: the Queen applauded. The
Prince and Stockmar wrote frequent detailed memoranda
on the moral principles involved; equally detailed memoranda were commissioned from all kinds of expert authori-

ties; the best possible tutors for a wide range of subjects were engaged. Everyone concerned collaborated to produce the perfect man and the ideal prince. Unfortunately this paragon was conceived in abstract terms; it scarcely occurred to anyone to study the nature of the child Albert Edward, Prince of Wales (he was given the title while still in the cradle), at whom all the massed batteries of learning were directed.

His natural gifts, which were considerable, were for the warmth and colour of social life. He was by nature open-hearted, understanding, charming, idle and hot-tempered, and he had neither taste nor talent for any sort of book learning. Yet the education to which he was subjected can only be described as cramming.

His first timetable was drawn up by Prince Albert himself. Albert Edward, then aged seven, was to receive nine lessons every day, three of an hour each in languages, six others of half an hour each, making a six-hour day in all. The nine subjects were: religion, English, writing, French, music calculating, German, drawing and geography. This sort of routine, made more burdensome as he grew older by the inclusion of a wider range of subjects, and with the hours growing longer, continued for something like eleven years. One or two very carefully selected Etonians crossed the river to Windsor Castle to make a sort of quorum at his lessons, but the idea that he might himself see something of the famous school or join in its recreations was rejected with horror.

As he grew towards adolescence it became clear that he would always be backward in intellectual attainment; he was naturally lazy, and even the rod, wielded by Prince Albert himself, could not drive knowledge into him. One of his instructors proposed drastic changes in the regimen: 'Make him climb trees! Run! Row! Ride! In many ways savages are much better educated than we.' But this advice—which might not have been thought so crazy at Gordonstoun a century later—came only from M. Velsin the French tutor, and was not to be taken seriously by the royal parents and the wise and weighty men to whom they turned for advice. Kicking against the pricks all the time, the Prince of Wales reached the age of seventeen speaking perfect German (the language of the home circle) and French; also English with a strong German accent, which never left him throughout life. All other academic subjects he had successfully resisted, though he loved serious music (as a listener, not an executant) and showed a considerable taste and talent for amateur acting.

The Prince Consort had set his heart on giving his adopted country something new in its history—a university man on the Throne. And the heir must enjoy the best that the combined academic resources of Great Britain could supply. So in the space of two years he was sent to no fewer than three universities—Edinburgh, Oxford and Cambridge. But there was no question of exposing him to the temptations of life in undergraduate society. In each seat of learning a large private house was taken for him, and there he went into residence for a term or two, with a full court staff of governor, tutor and equerries—one of the duties of the governor being to see that the Prince did not smoke.

He was not allowed to attend lectures in college; lecturers and their students must come to his house, and all must stand up when he entered the lecture room. He must not join undergraduate clubs, play undergraduate games, or accept undergraduate invitations. Her Majesty and the Prince expected him to entertain in a manner becoming to his rank; but this meant that the guests of the young man of nineteen or twenty must be heads of colleges, professors, and others of the most venerable figures of the university.

There was never any possibility of his attempting a degree.

His total acquisition of knowledge from the three universities combined would not have overburdened an average sixth-form boy of today. And of university life in the larger and more fruitful sense he was given scarcely a glimpse. When at last he went down and was gazetted to a commission in the Army, he plunged into military life as a heaven-sent escape, kicked over the traces, and soon became involved in a scandal that, in the Queen's horrified imagination, was mainly responsible for bringing down his father's by no means grey hairs with sorrow to the grave.

Edward VII was succeeded in 1910 by his second son, who not having become the heir until his brother's death when he was already adult had been educated as a sailor rather than as a future King. George V never doubted that a naval officer's training is the best possible preparation for kingship; and later the highly successful reign of his second son helped to give weight to the argument. In between these two comes the short reign of Edward VIII, the great-grandchild of Queen Victoria's old age, who from the moment of his birth was marked out as the twentieth-century's child of destiny, to be brought up from that moment as the future King.

Edward VIII, as the Duke of Windsor, has himself told the story of his youth. His father, he says, 'was a perfect expression of the Victorian and Edwardian eras . . . and had the Victorian's sense of probity, moral responsibility, and love of domesticity. He believed in God, in the invincibility of the Royal Navy, and the essential rightness of whatever was British.' He ruled 'that Bertie and I should be educated exactly as he and his elder brother had been'.

For the first year after Queen Victoria's death, in 1901 when Prince Edward was six and a half, he and his brother Albert ('Bertie') were taught by an Alsatian lady, Mlle Helen Bricka. The main subjects were French and German, though conversationally the boys had picked up the latter language simultaneously with English from their German nursemaid. It was, the Duke of Windsor recalls, 'the other important language of those days, the *Muttersprache* of many of our relations'. When he was nearly eight the two boys were handed over to a tutor, two years older than their father, whose name was Henry Peter Hansell. He was a graduate of Magdalen College, Oxford, and is remembered by his elder pupil as 'a typical English schoolmaster of the period. He had played football at Oxford, was a six-handi-cap golfer, and a crack rifle shot. He thus combined a mild scholarship with a muscular Christianity, accentuated by tweeds and an ever-present pipe. Needless to say, he was a bachelor.'

Mr. Hansell thought the boys ought to go and mix with their contemporaries at an ordinary preparatory school. That proposal, fifty years ahead of royal thinking, was over-ruled by their father; so instead Hansell organized their education on lines as close to those of a preparatory school of the time as was possible for only two pupils confined in a Palace. For disciplinary purposes the ultimate authority in the background was not a headmaster but 'Papa', to whose study they were summoned when necessary as if to the 'Captain's Cabin'.

Prince Edward had absorbed a perceptible element of the service spirit by the time he sat for the entrance examination for the Royal Naval College at Osborne. He passed in February 1907—indeed the Admiralty told his father he was the best boy they had examined that year—and for the next four years, first at Osborne and then at Dartmouth, he received exactly the same training as any other cadet destined to a seagoing career. He was still at Dartmouth when his grandfather King Edward died and he became immediately Duke of Cornwall. The following summer, after doing homage to his father at the Coronation on June

22, 1911, he was called upon to be the central figure in a unique pageant.

After Mr. Asquith, the Prime Minister, the most influential member of the Government was the Chancellor of the Exchequer, David Lloyd George. That most fervent of Welsh patriots had determined to gratify the national spirit of his countrymen by 'reviving' the traditional ceremony of the installation of a new Prince of Wales in the historic scene of Caernarvon Castle, where the first English Prince was said to have been proclaimed in 1284. In fact there was no tradition to revive; for six hundred years the Princes, if formally inaugurated at all, had been invested by the Sovereign in a private ceremony at Westminster or Windsor. That, however, did not confine the soaring imagination of Lloyd George. He entered into consultation with Dr. Edwards, the Archbishop of Wales; and they took advice from the Heralds, who provided them with a model in the ceremonial for the introduction of a new peer into the House of Lords. With this as a basis they devised between them a spectacular ritual of display, which was duly performed on a sweltering July day in the roofless but still stately ruins of Caernarvon Castle.

It was a splendid occasion, and undoubtedly stirred the hearts of the ten thousand Welshmen who were able to find places in the Castle garth to watch it. The pomp of it, however, was not much to the taste of the Prince, who had just passed out of Dartmouth and had developed the typical naval reticence and aversion from self-advertisement. He did not care much for dressing up, and when a little before the appointed day 'a tailor appeared to measure me for a fantastic costume designed for the occasion, consisting of white satin breeches and a mantle and surcoat of purple velvet edged with ermine, I decided things had gone too far. . . . What would my Navy friends say if they saw me in this preposterous rig? There was a family blow-up that night; but in the end my mother, as always, smoothed things over.

"You mustn't take a mere ceremony so seriously," she said. "Your friends will understand that as a Prince you are obliged to do certain things that may seem a little silly. It will be only for this once." '

In the end the Prince played his part with dignity and grace. After the Home Secretary, Winston Churchill, had 'mellifluously' proclaimed his titles, the King carried out the investiture. 'Upon my head he put a coronet cap as a token of principality, and into my hand the gold verge of government, and on my middle finger the gold ring of responsibility. Then, leading me by the hand through an archway to one of the towers of the battlements, he presented me to the people of Wales. Half fainting with heat and nervousness I delivered the Welsh sentences that Mr. Lloyd George, standing close by in the ancient garb of Constable [of Caernarvon] had taught me.'

Queen Elizabeth II, when she created her son Prince of Wales, promised the Welsh people that when he was grown up she would present him to them at Caernarvon. She did not, however, promise a repetition of the ceremony of 1911, which she agrees with her uncle was overblown even for its own time, and thinks would be certainly too pompous for the simpler royal way of life today. It was fabricated for the occasion and leaves the Queen and her advisers quite free to set it aside altogether or to prune it to suit the less ostentatious manners of her son's generation. It may be taken as reasonably certain that Prince Charles will not be compelled to wear the dress that so embarrassed his predecessor more than half a century ago.

With considerable relief after the formalities of Caernarvon, the Prince of Wales embarked in August in H.M.S. *Hindustan* for his first cruise as a midshipman. This lasted only three months, and was passed entirely in home waters. On his return he was summoned before his father, who informed him, to his great disappointment, that the Navy was

too specialized a career for one in his position. He must go
to the university—the first heir to the Throne in the history
of England to reside there as an ordinary undergraduate.
Mr. Hansell's steady pressure had at last overcome the King's
faith in the Navy as a royal education in itself. The Prince
was to be entered at Hansell's own old college, Magdalen;
and after a few months of travel in Europe, under his title of
Earl of Chester, he matriculated there in October 1912.

He came up well equipped to 'box a compass, read naval
signals, run a picket boat, and make cocoa for the officer of
the watch'—but with next to nothing of the school ground-
ing on which an Oxford education is ordinarily built. He
was, however, provided with tuition by the best scholars the
university possessed in the particular studies, legal, historical
and linguistic, which would be most useful to a future King;
they were headed by Sir William Anson, Warden of All
Souls, one of the greatest authorities on the British Constitution and government. To him the Prince read his weekly
essay. He did not read for a degree. But what Oxford had
done for him may be summarized in some sentences from
an account of his life there written by the President of
Magdalen, Sir Herbert Warren, in November 1914, by
which time the Prince had gone down and joined the
Grenadier Guards for service in the first world war:

'His essays, which at first were conscientious reproduc-
tions and compositions, became more and more his own,
both in thought and expression. In the end, though not yet
twenty and only at the age when many sixth-form boys are
just beginning Oxford, he acquired a considerable mastery.
Gifted with a good verbal memory, a freshness of view, and
decided independence of character, his essays, if not exactly
literary, became more and more interesting, and again and
again were striking and eloquent, if only in their genuine
sincerity and simple honesty.

'Bookish he will never be: not a "Beauclerk", still less a

"British Solomon". That is not to be desired, but the Prince of Wales will not want for power of ready and forcible presentation, either in speech or writing. And all the time he was learning more and more every day of men, gauging character, watching its play, getting to know what Englishmen are like both individually and in the mass.'

If a similar report can be rendered by the Master of Trinity College, Cambridge, when Charles Prince of Wales goes down there will be little to complain of in his education.

King Edward's brother the Duke of York, who became George VI, was not educated for the Throne. He probably did not think of his daughter as a future Queen before his own Accession, for at the time of the Abdication it is believed that his personal wish was to stand aside in favour of one of his younger brothers, not wanting to impose the heavy burden of the Crown upon a girl's shoulders.

However, he allowed himself to be persuaded, and at the age of ten Princess Elizabeth became Heiress Presumptive. At that time she had for three years been having lessons at home with a governess, Miss Marion Crawford, and it was several years more before any attempt was made to give her studies a specialized bent because of the position she would one day inherit.

A fairly detailed account of her educational progress was published by the present writer at the time of her coming of age in 1947. Her Majesty turns that account aside with gentle derision as an idealized picture, and even doubts whether she is entitled to call herself an educated woman at all. That, of course, is altogether excessive modesty. She does not possess, nor did any of her elders ever wish her to seek, the bluestocking erudition of Elizabeth I. She has nevertheless an extremely well-furnished mind, ranging easily and confidently over the whole field of human interest that the modern representative monarch needs to comprehend. In place of the allegedly overdrawn picture of 1947 it is perhaps permissible to quote a less detailed version from the same pen, published in 1958. After the elements had been acquired under Miss Crawford: 'other teachers were called in to give specialist help; teachers of dancing, of swimming, of music, and the Vicomtesse de Bellaigue to teach the princesses French. Still later the Provost of Eton, Sir Henry Marten, was asked to introduce Princess Elizabeth to such branches of knowledge as were particularly required for the equipment of a future Queen. But all alike were working under authority; it was not left to any of them to determine the general direction, or even the major details, of the princesses' education. That was shaped to a clearly conceived plan, which was framed by their mother. By comparison with the curricula of the leading girls' schools of that day or this, the plan would be considered somewhat old-fashioned; indeed Queen Mary, who was by temperament more inclined than her daughter-in-law to put a high value on strictly intellectual discipline, sometimes expressed her misgivings. But the Duchess of York had a definite idea of the sort of training she wished her daughters to receive, and pursued her course untroubled by other peoples' doubts. She desired them first to spend as much of their childhood as possible in the open air, and, however much in later life they might become involved in the pomp of cities, to learn to feel always at home in country surroundings and country pursuits. Then she would have them acquire good manners and perfect deportment, and to cultivate all of the distinctively feminine graces; for she is of those whose natural instinct is to emphasize the contrast between the sexes rather than seek to assimilate them to one another. She desired them to develop a civilized appreciation of the arts, and especially of music, in which she herself has some accomplishment. After care had been taken of these elements of a young lady's all-round education, the Duchess fully agreed that her children should gain as much reasonable book-learning as might prove to be within their capacity; but this she regarded as only one of several branches of education, to be kept in proper proportion with the rest and in subordination to the whole. When, for example, it became apparent that Princess Elizabeth would never progress beyond the simplest elements of mathematics, it did not worry the Duchess at all.'

This simple, traditional, ladylike course of education came to a turning-point after the battle of Dunkirk, when Princess Elizabeth was fourteen. From that time the threat of invasion, with the possibility, however remote, that the Heiress Presumptive might fall into the enemy's hands, had to be taken into account. Many children of her age were being sent by their parents to seek safety in Canada or the United States. But the King, with her own unhesitating concurrence, decided that such a withdrawal from danger was not for her: she was the representative of all the boys and girls of England and her duty was to share their perils. But it was thought best that the two princesses should be kept out of London, where the King and Queen coolly stood up to nine direct hits on Buckingham Palace by German bombs; and accordingly they took up their residence for the greater part of the war in Windsor Castle.

The Provost of Eton was called in to give Princess Elizabeth the special tuition that seemed important for a future Queen. Under him she studied history, with special emphasis on its constitutional and social aspects.[1]

1. To quote again from the work just cited:
'She was also taken carefully through the outlines of the history of the many nations belonging to the British Commonwealth and Empire, devoting substantial periods of time to the study of colonialism, and the evolution of colonies into sovereign states, and not shrinking from the austere but necessary subject of public finance in peace and war. The study of the past was made to merge into that of contemporary life, and for several years the hours set apart for discussion with the Provost on "Current Affairs" were used to focus the whole of her education on preparation for the tasks awaiting her at an unknown distance in the future.'

On her eighteenth birthday the emergency regulations required her to report at the Labour Exchange for service in aid of the war effort. An Act had just been passed making her eligible, though not yet of age, to be a Counsellor of State acting with others for the King when he was out of the country; and her father thought that the public duties which would now inevitably increase were in themselves a sufficient war work to satisfy her conscience. She herself, however, insisted that she wished to share the experience of other girls of her age, and persuaded him to grant her his commission as a second subaltern in the Auxiliary Territorial Service. This was in March 1945. Already, when the King went in July 1944 to visit his victorious troops in the Mediterranean, she had taken her place as a Counsellor of State, and her public career had begun.